THE ROAD, SO LONG

Paul Bethune

Above the Noise Publishing
Victoria, BC

© 2018 Paul Bethune. All rights reserved.

No part of this book may be used or reproduced in any manner whatsoever without the express written permission of the publisher or author. The exception would be in the case of brief quotations embodied in critical articles or reviews, and pages where permission is specifically granted by the publisher or author, or in the case of photocopying, a licence from Access Copyright, www.accesscopyright.ca, 1-800-893-5777, info@accesscopyright.ca.

Library of Canada Cataloguing in Publication data is available.

ISBN 978-0-9936367-3-8 (Hardcover Edition)
ISBN 978-0-9936367-0-7 (Paperback Edition)
ISBN 978-0-9936367-4-5 (E-book Edition)

First Edition Printing 2019

Editing by Lorraine Gane
Front cover image, illustrations, and hand-lettering by Laura Lavender
Book design by Clint Hutzulak, Rayola Creative

PRINTED AND BOUND IN CANADA

Published in Canada by Above the Noise, Victoria, bc www.abovethenoisepublishing.com.

For more information contact: publishing@abovethenoise.ca

Special discounts are available on quantity purchases by corporations, associations, and others. For details, contact the publisher at the address above.

For more information on the book and author please visit www.paulbethune.com

*To my wife Kimberly Robinson,
for your unwavering love and support.*

Contents

I

Reality	3
The Unparalleled Man	4
Pride (1)	5
Dried Flowers (1)	6
Bird in a Cage	7
The End, the Beginning	8
Changes (1)	9
Life Still Goes On	10
Building a World	11
Getting By	12
She	13
A Poem for Vicki	14
Sometimes	15
Death by a Stranger	17
Just Like Every Other Day	18
Only the Men	20
The Year I Grew Up	21
To Accept is to Be	23
Do You Still Think of Me?	24
You Were	25
Floating	26
Would You Still Cry at My Funeral?	27
Blame	28
I Had Forgotten How to Laugh	29
Incredible as it May Seem	30
My Empty Heart	31
My Child Who Was One	32
My Quiet One	33
Not Ever	34
Wasted Thought	35
No Together	36
Only Words	37
You Never Wipe Your Tears	38
Attitudes	39
This House	40
Looking at You	41
A New Creed	42
At Peace (1)	43

On This Day	44
My Spring	45
Dancing Flames	46
Doing the Right Thing	47
Footprints	48
Sleeping Flakes	49
To Excel	50
As I Lie Here Alone	51
The End	52
Waving Grass	53
Change of Heart	54
The Only Cure	55
Slim Jim	56
Ice Castles	57
Behind the Smile	58
One Snowflake, One Tear	59
In Silence	60
My Friend	61
A Matter of Time (I)	62
The Face of an Angel	63
Times	64
Open Window	65
Child of the Ocean	66

II

Past the Tears	71
Pride (II)	72
Indifference	73
Dying Breath	74
A Matter of Time (II)	75
Beside You	76
Once in My Life	77
Honesty and Tears	78
Changes (II)	79
Your Pain	80
In My Mind	81
To Capture the Moment	82
Advice	83
Lightning	84
Dragon's Jaws	85
The Building Which Destroys	86

Where to Turn?	87
Another Day	89
Apathy	90
Hmmm	91
How Bad Could it Be?	92
Losing It	93
Motivation	94
Longing	95
Serious	96
Bang	97
This is It	98
Deliverance	99
Seasons	100
Then and Now	101
Missing You	102
Enough is Enough	103
Say When	104
All I Need to Say	105
Blazing Eyes	106
Grief	107
Yesterday's Pain	108
All by Myself	109
The Kiss of Change	110
Sixth Sense	111
Surrender	112
What Are You Thinking?	113
The Essence of Change	114
The Building of Trust	115
Influence	116
The Word (1)	117
Anticipation	118
Friends	119
What's Wrong?	120
Out of My Mind	121
My World	122
A Song for You	123
Just as Well	125
Some Space	126
In Your Eyes	127
This Day in Your Life	128
Summit	129
The Power of Words	130
One Event	131

The Other Side	132
Today	133
Back in Touch	134
The Note	135
Looking Ahead	136
At Peace (II)	137
Looking Back	138
What to Do?	139
A Year Ago Today	140
Failure	141
Anyone	142
As Simple as That	143
The Wound of Time	144
One Day You Awaken	145
In Case You've Forgotten	146
A Time	147

III

Moments	151
The Cure	152
Unrelenting	153
Special	154
Time to Row	155
Lifetimes	156
Alone	157
Sparks	158
Instincts	159
Plus ça change	160
Signals	161
Upstream	162
The Real Thing	163
Check-Out Time	164
Just Another Day	165
Yours	166
The Challenge	167
Attitude	168
Numbness	169
Nothing	170
No Longer	171
Earth, Wind and Fire	172
The Journey	173

Finally	174
Last Night	175
Why You	176
…And Then Some	177
The Last Night	178
The Word (II)	179
Human	180
Helium	181
Closure	182
Waiting	183
Not Because of Him	184
On the Beach	185
Wonder	186
Words of Peace	187
Dried Flowers (II)	188
Holly	189
Destiny	190
This Torch	191
I Just Am	192
No Idea	193
You're Back	194
Always Does	195
What You Give	196
Lake Holly	197
Together…Forever	198
At Times Like These	199
The Measure of a Man	200
Time	201
Thanks for Being You	202
Love	203
My Philosophy	204

IV

Truth	209
Stages	210
Just Right	211
The Perfect One	212
Once Again	213
Praying for the Storm	214
Why Can't I?	215
Faith	216

Blessed	217
Soul	218
A Tear	219
Christmas Dreams	220
Waiting	221
A Story Book Finish	222
Any Addiction	223
Trust	224
Then and Now	225
Fate	226
The Road, So Long	227
Stranger	228
Breath of Fresh Air	229
Pleasure	230
Because	231
My Hearth	232
Know	233
Oasis	234
Senses	235
Thoughts	236
Written Over Time	237
Loving Kim	238
A Gift	239
Day Dreams	240
For the Moment	241
Away	242
More and More	243
Acknowledgements	246
About the Author	247

I

Reality

What appears to exist rarely does,
What one wants to exist rarely does,
What seems apparent is obscured in disregard.

Is it reality that occurs in day dreams and make beliefs?
Is it reality sought by all in life's ambitions?
Is it reality seen in the faces of those who
Sense reality for the first time?

Does one seek reality when he's content otherwise?
Does one hear reality when he listens
Only to what he wishes to hear?
Does one speak of reality
When he desires to draw only from his dreams?

Nothing is more painful than facing reality
Rather than continuing to thrive on fantasies and blind truths.

Observation should be heeded by those on the outside,
To fulfill you with life as it is on the inside.

1975

The Unparalleled Man

Cradling the small babe,
He is a giant in station.
His love and generosity are unending,
Which lends itself to the raising of
A receptive human being.
Direction and understanding ever present
Molds one so certain, one so sensitive
There is influence so great, so constant
Yet accepted with boundless joy,
A man so humble
He is the man, the unparalleled man.
I love you Dad.

1975

Pride (I)

Forever is a long time to ponder,
What could be has surely not died.
Yet, we must consider so carefully,
Can we live on only our pride?

To say "late is better than never,"
Would surely rule out any blame.
As always, I'll love you forever,
But I am saddened you don't feel the same.

Our thoughts are blurred while in anger.
It's so easy to don fits of rage.
Can we suddenly turn that old page?

Can our true feelings be nonexistent?
Can the love in our hearts be denied?
A fool would be too persistent.
A greater fool has only pride.

February 1980

Dried Flowers (I)

I am dried flowers
A never-ending look of life,
Yet have ceased to subsist.
Appealing, yet unnatural.
Present, yet uneventful.
I cannot weep for fear of destruction
I cannot blossom and be vulnerable.
I am content, needing no stimulus.
I am simply here giving life to nothing else.
The wind is my enemy carrying change and unrest.
A crumbling world begins to unfold.
Yet no one can tell.
I know this so well.
I need nothing.

December 1981

Bird in a Cage

I have often felt like a bird in a cage,
Yearning for escape, yet content in my world.
Desired control, relative to circumstances,
Controlling what enters as a means
For coping with the unknown.
Preparing for what lies ahead.

The past is so clear, I have always been here.
The present I've met as a light silhouette.
The future uncertain till the draw of a curtain
In the cage I respect, for the world I neglect.

When changes occur, there's a bend in the bar.
I begin my escape, but only so far.
A relative newness unfamiliar to me
Is blinding my concept of what I can and can't see.

This new world I find must not leave me behind.
My wings spread completely, I explore so discreetly
To the world beyond, one of poise, grace and lust
Assembled in one, in one whom I trust.

The cage again waits providing strength so secure.
I re-enter for now no longer unsure.

I am a bird in a cage.

December 1981

The End, the Beginning

Enthralled in bitterness,
Unbecoming, yet undeniably present.
This cannot be altered,
For the present inflicting.
Time is the only hope for a cure
Of a wound so profound it baffles.
Only a prevailing sense of relief
Rescues me from tragedy.
It is the end, yet it is the beginning.
One life ceases, but another must go on.
One can only reflect as one considers the past.
And one can only be optimistic for the future.

Ah, the future.
I am blessed with youth.
I am gaining wisdom.
So held back by the past
Only to catapult into the future.
I am waiting.
I am patient.
I am prepared.
Toughened by doom,
Rejoiced by the unknown.
My senses await.
The tenses are great.

December 1981

Changes (I)

I had always believed people could change.
Finding the ingredients for making the change,
Is what life is all about.
If finding the ingredients makes you a gourmet,
I couldn't boil water right now.

January 8, 1982

Life Still Goes On

The death of a soul
Is a devastation beyond comprehension.
My insides are in a state of collapse,
Yet they can only collapse so much.
The hurt will end,
But I am not thinking of the future.
I can only dwell on my present sorrow,
A feeling of absolute emptiness
Lives where my soul once was.
At least there is no fear of uncertainty.
Things have never been so obvious.
That which has hurt me should not be sought after.
Yet a return to myself
Requires the pursuit of something unobtainable.
The consummation of life's ironies have
Given birth to an unhappiness so profound
Joy has become a dream.
My motivation has ceased.
My happiness, nonexistent.
My direction is absent.
My heart barely beats.
But life still goes on.

April 6, 1982

Building a World

Disappointment is no one's fault but our own.
We create our hopes and build our expectations.
Suddenly anticipation becomes devastation,
As a justification of the means.
This is the end.
Now what does it mean?
We must be self-reliant.
Expect nothing and anything will seem fantastic.
Never let a closeness to anything develop.
The risks are too great.
The disappointment just waits.
Create an atmosphere comprised of yourself,
Then the world becomes you, because you are the world.
And you are the creator of life: good, bad, happiness
And sorrow in that world.
There will be no need for second guessing.
No possibility of the unexpected.
Because you know yourself well enough,
And remember,
You are expecting nothing.
Surround yourself with simple yet meaningful pleasures,
Things which are time consuming, inspiring,
But most of all controlled by none but yourself.
You hold the key.
You open your own doors.
Become an entity so impregnable
That fear of collapse seems impossible.
Be elusive, yet reachable.
Reject no one, yet remain evasive.
Above all, avoid vulnerability
Lest you desire defeat of something which takes time, effort
And self-composure to create.
Remembering to expect nothing
You have achieved everything.

April 6, 1982

Getting By

What seemed right all along
One day tells you it's wrong.
Something finally did catch your eye.
Now we have separate hearts.
We explore different charts.
Well that's fine 'cause I know I'll get by.

Once we were afraid
Of the plans we had made.
Poor timing I cannot deny.
It was a cold winter's day,
That's all I can say.
We'll no longer live out this lie.
Tenth day of December,
I shall always remember,
It was over, you started to cry.
We pledged our lost souls,
And set our own goals
Because we knew in our hearts we'd get by.

But remember all the things you said,
Because you know what you mean, as do I.
And without me to guide you, can't see inside you.
And I know you will never get by.

June 6, 1982

She

An individual worthy of consideration as she enters a room.
She has a surface freshness which cannot be denied.
Yet few, if any, understand her internal makeup.
Long ago she was an individual of strength and dedication,
A dedication so overpowering it was difficult to handle.
And indeed, it was poorly handled.

There was a dedication for one whom had never been dedicated.
A great sense of pride, that too, broken by one with only false pride.
There are oddities though resulting in the destruction
Of an already fragile structure.
Explanations could never be enough.
She has always been suspect and falls into her own trap.
She has always been loving,
Yet she has destroyed an entity existing on false pretense anyway.
She has lost her sensitivity
But that breeds a certain toughness,
Which in turn develops a new sense of pride.
She has changed a life of contentment into one of confusion, anger
And frustration.
Yet she is loved.
She questions stability, oddly enough for one with no dogma.

Forgotten dedication, now driven by whim.
I am forgotten, she has gone to him.
I have been dealt a favour, that fact I shall savour.
The world is now mine, there is nothing to bind.
Old feelings resisted, she has never existed.

June 21, 1982

A Poem for Vicki

So young and naïve
The wisdom you are gaining and shall gain takes time.
Experience is so vital too.
There will be bumps and bruises along the way.
But the healing process is like no other.
You can reflect on and draw from the events in your life.
It rewards you with wondrous decision-making.
Never be ashamed of your previous actions,
They are history.
How they affected others should be of little concern.
You must constantly call on your assets,
Of which you have many:
Your unending caring attitude,
Your pleasing physical appearance,
Your humour that uplifts the lowest of lows.
Never be ashamed of anything you have done.
Only draw on all which you have to offer.

August 22, 1982

Sometimes

You know I still think of you…
Sometimes.
Reflection is a wonderful thing…
Sometimes.
I look back and ponder our lives together
And our lives apart.
Sometimes I smile 'cause it brings me joy to
Know we spent even a second together.
Yet sometimes it brings tears,
Probably because I think of the wasted years
Which should have been our most productive,
Fulfilling and rewarding.
I think they were…
Sometimes.
Naturally we have grown through interaction.
Self-awareness and unprecedented self-respect
Have emerged like a flower
Blooming at mid-morning,
Stretching outward, grasping at all that shall
Feed it and perpetuate it.
It is a beautiful act.
Yet openness inspires vulnerability.
This in addition to a valuable experience…
Sometimes.
It is an openness we never shared.
Strength through devastation like I never
Thought possible occurred.
But the devastation lingers…
Sometimes.
But just as the flower has been awarded air,
Warmth and sunlight,
I, too, have been the benefactor of wondrous things:
Self-discipline, self-motivation and unbelievable
Self-confidence,
At least its beginnings are rooted there,
Surface aesthetics leads to self-assurance which in
Turn lends itself to fantastic inner satisfaction.
With newly acquired wisdom and self-assuredness,

You'd think I would negate a detrimental past,
But was it so bad?
I guess not 'cause I still think of you…
Sometimes.

1982

Death by a Stranger

No sign of danger
As my life drew to a close.

When he approached me
My pen well in hand,

He said "Excuse me,"
"I'm sorry, you are dead."

Then he walked away
And I fell into the sand.

I looked up for an instant
My world was passing by
Just over forty
I'm too young to die.

I gave myself to the people of the world,
I sang my songs again and again,
I wrote of you all as seen through my eyes,
Won't you think of me now and then?

January 6, 1983

Just Like Every Other Day

I thought of you today
Just like every other day.
This time I was simply waiting for a bus.
I tried to consider the significance of that,
But I put it out of my mind,
Just like every other day.

I wanted you today
Just like every other day.
My desire for you is ever increasing.
I can only think of the two of us together,
But I put it out of my mind,
Just like every other day.

I needed you today
Just like every other day.
You are my strength and salvation
I cannot go on without you near,
But I put it out of my mind,
Just like every other day.

I love you today
Just like every other day,
Love that fills my soul like nothing else.
I contemplate its aimlessness,
But I put it out of my mind,
Just like every other day.

I hated you today
Just like every other day.
Blaming you for my self-defeat,
Thinking you forced my destruction,
But I put it out of my mind,
Just like every other day.

But then….
I held you today
Not like any other day.
I know it was the last caress,
Wondering if we'd ever be as one,
And I can't get it out of my mind,
Just like every other day.

January 8, 1983

Only the Men

There have always been men who thought they could change
The world.
Times are so difficult, with oppression, segregation, recession
And prejudice.
Lenin fought to deliver his people an equal society,
But he is dead now.
Lincoln freed all of the slaves,
But he is dead now.
Hitler waged war and prosperity,
But he is dead now.
Chaplin raised money and hopes,
But he is dead now.
King gave us speeches and education,
But he, too, is now dead.
There have always been men who could change the world,
Yet they are all dead now.
This new generation of men who can change the world will one
Day be dead too.
So, you see...the world will never change,
Nothing changes.
Only the men.

January 8, 1983

The Year I Grew Up

I have always gotten more out of life than I put in.
And nothing bothered me, simply because nothing bothered me.
But then came 1982,
The year I grew up.

In the past I had learned a great many things.
I learned the pain of love,
Felt the emergence of self-confidence,
The tragedy of my family slipping away.
The devastation of losing a girl whose love I shall never
Know again.
It was some year,
It was the year I grew up.

The toughest part is that all of the people from whom I drew
Strength are now drawing from me.
I had taken their guidance for granted.
Now they turn to me for direction.
It was nice to be needed last year,
It was the year I grew up.

It was a year of gain and losses.
I lost poise, patience and people.
I gained respect, responsibility and reassurance.
It was a year I won't soon forget.
It was the year I grew up.

I feel like all of the pressures of the world
Are on my shoulders.
But I am so well off.
I eat every day.
I have people who love me.
I can walk, talk, see, feel, hear and taste.
I did not lose those special things,
In the year I grew up.

I've gained wisdom and new friends.
I'm moving upwards in my vocation.
I've given up on lost hopes and dreams.
I have become a realist.
And just think...
It all happened,
In the year I grew up.

It seems like a decade.
That which has led me to my present state.
Three hundred and sixty-five of the finest.
Bringing challenge after challenge,
Testing my maturity, conviction and strength.
Yet I ask myself. Why am I so different?
I know.
It was the year I grew up.

January 27, 1983

To Accept is to Be

ow I feel today
is as every other day,
A myriad of emotions.
Feeling happiness,
given to sadness.
Just sensitive, I guess.
It makes me yearn for older times,
older attitudes and previous circumstance.
But to be realistic is to accept today,
not desire yesterday.
For yesterday is gone,
the future is tomorrow,
and I must be able to accept all that it brings.
Should circumstance fail to enlighten my world,
let me bring joy to others.
To give and give shall make life important
once again,
An importance I've missed, a direction I've lost.
My outlook's been altered,
so have I.
I just need to accept that…

February 12, 1983

Do You Still Think of Me?

I wonder sometimes,
Do you still think of me?

Do you still think of me when
You see a familiar profile?
You want to have a closer look,
But you really hope it isn't me.

Do you still think of me when
You hear a certain song?
You want it to play forever,
But you never want to hear it again.

Do you still think of me when
He touches you a certain way
Running his fingers gently up your spine?
You wish I was there to continue,
But in your heart you're glad it's him.

Do you still think of me when
You say a certain thing I once said?
You smile, about to say "It's funny
How we think alike,"
But you hope you never say it again.

Do you still think of me when
A familiar fragrance penetrates your very soul?
You take a deep breath to savour a dying memory,
But you hope to avoid it in the future.

When you are sitting alone
And your senses are sharp,
Alive and inviting, I wonder
What you think of then?
Do you still think of me?

February 14, 1983

You Were

I've tried to think of what you have meant to me,
Not in terms of emotional upheaval, but humanistic growth.
I've tried to think of what you were.
You were my introduction to manhood in the rustic sense.
You were the cause for an emerging caring attitude.
You were frustration in its gravest sense.
All of these things were and are important.
Unfortunately, through our sharing of time, I have not learned
What I desire, but have realized what I must not attach myself
To in the future.
It's a perplexing intermixing of systematic analysis.
There was so much I loved and so much I detested,
But I have but one regret:
We never took it to the end.
This shall haunt me for a lifetime.
It is my only motivation for desire of your return.
There is so much I wish to tell you, right now, all of it hurting.
So it shall go untold.
The worst of it is,
You almost got me to participate in the growth of an ego already
Too extended.
I tried little to enhance it, and I should have torn it apart.
It might have made you a little more human.
It shall be your greatest enemy, but you'll realize that too late.
You need me much more than I need you.
But that's okay, 'cause you'll never realize it
And I shall never offer it.
It's a shame, but it's only because…
Of what you were.

April 30, 1983

Floating

I am sitting here alone today,
Not uncommon, yet something is different.
Everything is in darkness, but the sun is shining.
Only silence can be heard above the blaring music.
I have no thoughts, yet my mind is racing.
I am floating above the grass's reach,
But it tickles my neck.
My thirst is insatiable, as brook water drips from my chin.
I am oblivious to essence, as I inhale to fulfillment.
There is total escape, but my senses are alive.
Just a dream versus reality…
I pray there is no winner.

May 22, 1983

Would You Still Cry at My Funeral?

I spend a great deal of time wondering what you think of me.
Are you bitter from a dissolving relationship no longer shared?
Do you hate the memories which plague you from time to time?
Are you stunned my presence no longer exists?
Do bad rumours become truth when you hear about me?
Is there a building resistance, hate and lack of concern?
You know, none of it matters to me at all.
I guess what it all comes down to is…
Would you still cry at my funeral?

June 1, 1983

Blame

All we do now is blame each other.
It's over, so why perpetuate the agony.
Nothing matters concerning us,
Because there is no us,
Only two people trying not to blame themselves,
When there is no one else to blame.
Once we had such selfless values.
Indeed, an innocent reaction to emotional outcry.
We needed something from each other,
But I don't know what or why.
I only regret we wasted so many years of our youth.
Yet it spawned our adulthood.
We wanted everything,
Yet we are left with nothing…
Only blame.

June 24, 1983

I Had Forgotten How to Laugh

I had forgotten how to laugh
Until I stopped seeing you.
I have been too serious.
My heart now follows my head every day.
I had forgotten how to laugh.
Now I know no other way.

June 24, 1983

Incredible as it May Seem

There is a great deal of strangeness in my life.
I am beginning to know myself again.
Yet I feel sadness as I become what I have strived for.
I am a thousand miles from home, in a strange town.
Yet I continue to hold onto a love no longer in my grasp.
I must battle my prejudice to aid those I love.
Life's major problems go unsolved.
This is a bad dream.
I am really happy,
As incredible as it may seem.

June 28, 1983

My Empty Heart

What I feel in my heart
has been secured over time.
It is though my heart is translucent
and light has become thought,
and thought has become darkness.
It is a curious state which seeks no answers,
for a dogmatic heart which seeks no change.
It is my head giving rise to incredulity,
but my fervid heart emasculates logic.
Yet this once full heart
bleeds from purpose…
as it does from emptiness.

June 28, 1983

My Child Who Was One

In my mind's eye
while out for a run
on this very day,
I saw my child who was one.
Just children ourselves,
we had it undone.
The wrong decision
for our child who was one.
He bounced on my knee,
good God it was fun.
The smile of smiles
from my child who was one.
It was time for a walk,
but there was too much sun
so the carriage lid covered
my child who was one.
The cake was presented,
my pride weighed a ton.
But the flame was extinguished,
as was my child who was one.
The dream was of happiness,
but reality said shun.
The memory of my child,
my child who was one.

July 10, 1983

My Quiet One

I long to learn what lies behind those staring eyes.
I hope the reflections are happy,
but I fear the past clouds any happiness.
All you need is time, love and attention,
which I will provide so willingly.
We both are trying to negate the past,
for similar reasons, which will become our bond.
I'll change your thoughts from cloudy to sun,
behind the eyes
of my quiet one.

July 27, 1983

Not Ever

You cannot haunt me,
but you do.
You cannot force my hand,
but you do.
I have become my own person
with the exception of you.

Your existence obstructs my point of view.

Not now, nor will you ever
get what you want.
If it is me…
I have never been more correct.

August 18, 1983

Wasted Thought

I'm a little bit down right now.
There's a reason I cannot deny.
An unborn excuse brings sweat to my brow.
The sweat joins a tear which wells in my eyes.
I have to think clearly.
My mind cannot race,
Yet I would love so dearly,
To give him his natural place.

The question is to be or not…
But my mind is too clouded by wasted thought.

August 18, 1983

No Together

I'd asked you to be mine,
I promised all would be so fine,
But then you looked the other way.

I spent months being myself,
I put the world up on a shelf,
And now you're wanting me today.

I'd built the problems we shared,
Together we had never cared.
I only wonder what went wrong,
I guess we've known it all along.

There's you and there's me, no together,
No us and that's just fine,
But somehow I knew we'd weather
The storm we left behind.

We made promises meant to keep,
But we've just jumped in much too deep,
Now take a look at where we are.

You've become a stranger,
It's safe to say "our love's in danger."
Our separate ways have split too far.

August 24, 1983

Only Words

I was building a world,
but what happened?
I began to care again.
Oh how costly old attitudes are.

I was building a world,
with an unpayable debt.
My past is the currency,
they will not accept.

I tried to build a lifetime
on a mood, on a whim.
I had myself fooled,
now I'm out on a limb.

I should have remained
in my cage with the birds.
My God, I didn't realize,
they were only words.

August 18, 1983

You Never Wipe Your Tears

I'm not blind to your feelings,
I know what you face.
The problems are too deeply rooted,
For my input to erase.

They are all pent up,
I speak of your fears.
Yet, I have always wondered
Why you never wipe your tears.

August 31, 1983

Attitudes

I am standing in a very large room.
This room is filled with people.
No one is handicapped.
No one's colour is recognizable.
No religion is distinguishable.
There are no political ideals.
The sexes are undetermined.
We are all the same in this particular room.
There is only one imperfection—

The room is in total darkness.

September 20, 1983

This House

I am confused in this house.
It represents my present,
and holds my future.
It has an expanse of many rooms,
yet I have never felt so hemmed in.
It is a house full of orators,
but there is no communication.
It is filled with genuine love,
but animosity reigns supreme.

Life has become a contradiction
as I'm driven from all I've dreamed,
forced to face all I have done.
Solace is found outside these walls,
but all my joy lies within.
At a time when I need the most direction
I cannot focus on a single track.

I need a change,
when all I have done is change.
I must step lightly,
as the house which crushed my world
is itself too fragile to absorb my views.
I cannot deal with this new house…
I simply live in it.

October 21, 1983

Looking at You

Looking at you
I build a world from tears and sadness.
I only think of joy and gladness.
I feel this way every time…
I'm looking at you.

Looking at you,
I understand what poets mean.
I know what lovers have seen.
I have no reason nor rhyme…
I'm looking at you.

Looking at you
Our whole future bodes well.
We'll do all the things we should.
I simple feel sublime…
I'm looking at you.

Looking at you
I see him in your eyes.
He's our pride although he cries.
We'll be together all the time…
I'm looking at you.

December 1, 1983

A New Creed

I have run out of poems.
The words lie away
Tucked in my mind,
With nothing to say.
I'll seek them forever,
Those meaning so much,
My creed shall be written.
I'll live by it as such.

December 14, 1983

At Peace (I)

At last I am at peace with the world
As I lay beneath the frozen grass.
I need not respond to commands,
I need not do justice to society.
I can only be absolved by my maker.
I hope he saw my world, as I did.

December 14, 1983

On This Day

On this day late in the year,
My fate is decided,
My destiny is clear.
I'll treasure this day,
Which joins our two souls
As we meet with the future,
And reach for our goals.

December 15, 1983

My Spring

Lo this sleeping forest
bare from winter's fury
whose morning provides a white dew.

An eastern breeze removes new beauty
so short-lived in this barren wood.

Oh forest,
I rest in your crackling branches for now,
secure in the knowledge my spring shall defeat the wind.

January 20, 1984

Dancing Flames

As I look at your dancing colours,
I see a thousand other worlds
any of which I'd rather be a part.
Your images reflect my soul,
you dance to life from air.

But as I live and breathe
in this confusion,
I cannot grow.
Still, you dance and dance and dance.

January 23, 1984

Doing the Right Thing

It's an unfortunate upbringing
which molds a moral outlook.
You get the impression society
is always looking in.
Couple this with an immature fantasy,
and what is the result?
What else,
but doing the right thing.

It's insufficient reward
for a sacrifice as long as life.
What I prayed for yesterday,
no longer applies.
I simply forgot I didn't want it any more.

Now I am reminded with every passing second
of every passing day.
The intermittent smiles
do not justify this existence,
this existence…
based on the premise
of doing the right thing.

January 26, 1984

Footprints

These footprints in the snow
tell a lot about where I've been,
but provide no direction I may follow.
I can choose a new route in an instant,
but these footprints are always there
to tell me where I've been.

If my life is simply footprints in the snow,
I pray the wind fills them in,
so when I look back, I shall see nothing.
Realizing there will only be the new ones I make
and not the old ones impeding my direction.

Again, I quickly turn around
and there are footprints
always footprints…
in the snow.

March 23, 1984

Sleeping Flakes

The sky is a white silky blanket.
Such beauty could not be the enemy of day-to-day living.
Yet all the activity the sky sponsors for now
Simply becomes a curious immobile mass.
We're faced with all this confusion
Simply because of a trillion sleeping flakes.

March 30, 1984

To Excel

This metal dove takes me from a war-torn existence,
Bringing peace and tranquillity to a tattered soul.
Sleepy lakes among mountainous ranges
Are looming ominously under this path of flight.
A sudden white darkness obscures an appreciative eye,
Rapidly descending to end the dream,
And triggers my thinking about the purpose of my journey—

To excel.

May 22, 1984

As I Lie Here Alone

This darkness blinds my vision
as my feelings reach a peak.
I cannot see my hands,
as they barely grasp a crumpling world.
I cannot see my feet,
although I know I stand alone.
I cannot see my heart,
yet the relentless beating reminds me of its presence.
I cannot see my arms,
outstretched in search of an answer.
I cannot see my legs,
but they walk and walk,
        delivering me from this craziness.
I must clear my mind,
but my thoughts will not be ignored
as I lie here
alone.

May 24, 1984

The End

At last relief fills my body
overruled by nothing or no one.
I have helped to create this end
and I shall revel in its rewards.

There will be hurt.
There will be despair.
But I have the blessings of those who matter.

Yet the real responsibilities begin now.
These shall stem from the demands of the system,
to the reality of my self-indulgence.

However,
my freedom carries strings.
My future cannot be called my own.
Yet this is a new beginning,
because at last I have accepted…
the end.

May 31, 1984

Waving Grass

Waving grass welcomes me to frolic and hide,
to lay down in its softness is to find security,
if only for a moment.
This ocean of green does not argue with the wind,
it simply waves…
pleading with me to experience its freedom.

June 28, 1984

Change of Heart

It's difficult to explain why I want out.
There is really nothing wrong with you.
It's the situation.
I simply cannot cope with a relationship.

You feared that from the beginning.
I guess this only proves you right.

A husband, a father —
I simply can't play the part.
I can only say "I am sorry"
For this change of heart.

November 22, 1984

The Only Cure

Death is not such a bad thing
If it rescues one from a fate worse than it.
I wonder how something so easily employed
Is so difficult to accept when granted by one's own hand.
It's a definite sickness to consider an act so drastic,
But the situation causes the illness
And implies self-destruction as the only cure.
It's a shame, but it's the only decision
You never have a chance to regret.

December 20, 1984

Slim Jim

Slim and trim, that's our boy Jim,
We all like to look at him.
He's shown us so much discipline.
He used a diet, didn't use a gym
He's slim and trim, he's our boy Jim.

His sense of humour out on a limb,
But he still thinks life ain't all that dim.
It will be worth it for our boy Jim.
He'll have no excess 'round the rim.
He's slim, he's trim, that's our boy Jim.

I know he's excited to the brim.
His life now filled with vigour and vim.
It's off the bod he's had to skim,
Yes we are surely proud of him.
He's slim, he's trim, he's our boy Jim.

January 2, 1985

Ice Castles

I long for my journey to the ice castles.
I await the coolness, the solitude and the serenity they offer.

The crisp clear sparkle shall enlighten my senses
and provide me with awareness of my present surroundings.

The isolation shall grant my sanity,
so I need not cope with anything.

The quiet shall absorb the screams of my soul.

The journey will be long and arduous,
but ice castles promise rewards beyond imagination.

I wait.

January 22, 1985

Behind the Smile

I face every day with this expression.
It remains unchanged
by events of sadness or joy.
I cannot reveal my true feelings
so my innermost thoughts are imprisoned
behind the smile.

January 29, 1985

One Snowflake, One Tear

A snowflake on my cheek during a brisk walk.
I laughed aloud, yet felt awkward
As I revelled in this moment of childlike repose
With Mother Nature.

This one snowflake
Released me from all the worries and responsibilities
That have labelled my self-indulgence.

As it melted on my skin
It became a tear.
A visible one.

January 31, 1985

In Silence

Our recent silence has made things serious.
The tension I feel is incredible.
I suppose we never should have stopped joking.
It gave reality a chance it never deserved.

I can only wish this were another time,
A time before commitments and responsibilities.

Since nothing of significance shall ever occur
I can only dream of missing what I never had.

Your eyes are like those of a fawn
Watchful of the pursuit I cannot make.

I cannot demean the respect I have for you
By assuming the uncertain, by grasping at the unreachable.

I would give it all up for you…

All I need is a sign
You might consider me
Worthy of being a part of your life.

For now the silence holding the tension
Shall deliver no regrets.
For there are no regrets…
In silence.

February 18, 1985

My Friend

This paper I may call my friend,
has no shoulder to cry on.
Yet, I have no tears, only words,
And my friend shall absorb them all.

This friend can offer no advice,
For I do not wish to listen.
It sponsors no arguments,
It only reflects my views.

It never turns away.
It only awaits my script.

I had longed for a friend I could call "my best,"
When all along these scraps had awaited my call.

March 7, 1985

A Matter of Time (I)

It's only a matter of time
Before I gather my thoughts
And relieve myself of this life.
The comfort of darkness is elusive.
Yet it never leaves my soul.
Dreams of destruction envelope my sleep.
But for now they are only that.
Action will provide all the answers.
But I still wait.
Things aren't that bad.
Besides…
We've got to give life
The benefit of the doubt.

March 7, 1985

The Face of an Angel

The face of an angel envelops my mind's eye.
Her image prevails above all thought.
I long for the culmination of our bodies and souls.

But the image must fade
To restore my mind to peace.

My heart beckons me to say the words which I cannot.
The words have never come easily,
But I fear they will be spoken.

Time has become an enemy,
And distance shall prove no friend.
My memory shall ignore the time and miles,
As I miss,
The face of an angel.

March 26, 1985

Times

There are times when I anticipate greatness from you and me.
But you never seem to try,
And I really don't care.

There are times when the world seems like it's ours.
But it's still not good enough for you,
And I really don't want it.

There are times when our eyes are so wide open,
But you fail to see the light,
And I only mask my intent.

There are times when we seem to love each other,
But it's a convenience for you,
And just bad timing for me.

There are times when we should give it up,
But you would not know how,
And my cowardice leaves me mute.

Who do we think we are kidding?
Only ourselves,
And we could not even agree on that at the same time.

September 9, 1985

Open Window

This silent curtain
is still and in control...
until the open window presents a gusty foe
ruffling its enviable composure.

Alas, this curtain,
now still,
shields my view from an outside world,
with which I can no longer deal.

I cannot help but feel
my life constantly flows past an open window
when all I desire is to be
still and
silent and
undisturbed.

November 22, 1985

Child of the Ocean

My child of the ocean
your desert island has saved my soul.

I am adrift in search of answers,
but your sandy welcome
puts my granular thoughts to rest.

I am faced with the instinct to escape,
when I know I should not try.

You're my child of the ocean,
please never wave goodbye.

December 3, 1985

II

Past the Tears

What I must say,
can no longer go unsaid.
What I must do,
can no longer go undone.

Words and actions
have lain dormant for years.
Please hear me.
Please watch me.

Now I must get past the tears.

April 22, 1986

Pride (II)

When I look back on your life as told by you
I have a tremendous amount of pride in you.
You have accomplished everything I have yet to face.
You have provided all of the tools I need.
You have given me direction, example, guidance
And you have shared your experiences, so I may learn.

I think I am doing okay.

When we part
As one day we must
I shall live with only one hope —

That I have earned your pride.

July 25, 1986

Indifference

A strange indifference of late,
I trust I have caught in time.
People always expect me to be a certain way.
This natural, but
I can only keep this up for so long.
I know I made my own bed.
The problem is…
I am not sleeping very comfortably right now.

April 8, 1987

Dying Breath

I cannot cry for you
Though what I have seen brings tears.

I cannot pray for you
As I do not know your name.

I cannot feel empathy
For curiosity fills my soul.
I can only deal with it in retrospect,
And the effect it has had on me.

God, I am selfish.
When I think of how you lay
While God awaits your dying breath.

April 27, 1987

A Matter of Time (II)

I need no words here.
The heading speaks for itself.

God let me have the discipline
To live by what I say.

May 7, 1987

Beside You

I am sorry it has been so long
That since I have seen you
I need not be here
As you fill my dreams and thoughts each day.

My years have doubled since your passing,
But you gave enough of yourself to last a lifetime.

As you lie here in peace
Know I miss you.
And I look forward to the day
When it is not above you I kneel,
      But beside you I stand.

June 15, 1987

Once in My Life

I have loved once in my life.
It started the day I met you.
I die a little each day,
Knowing I cannot express my thoughts.
You don't even know me, one day you said.
Yet I would expend all of life's energies
To make that untrue.
You are so close,
Yet forever may describe the distance between us.
One of us must speak so the fantasy dies
Or reality takes hold.
If I love what I do not even know.
God would provide me no words to describe my feelings
If I knew you complete.

July 31, 1987

Honesty and Tears

It was gruesome,
The night of honesty and tears.
The words were irreparable,
It was a tale with no happy end.

I would have thought rational
People could iron out a solution,
But the force of words forged a greater divide.

I'm not sure where to go from here,
Since things will never be the same,
Yet nothing has changed for the moment.

It was wrong to think getting past the tears
Was all that confronted me.
It is nonreaction that
Will continue to force my hand.

God give me the strength
To play my hand as wise
And not in force.

Patience, as always
Must overpower frustration.

September 11, 1987

Changes (II)

It was a year of change,
But not for the better.
My assertions did not bring
The solutions I prayed they would.
However, the future looks different
And change is as good as a rest
Till I make the biggest change.
It was only a sentence away.
Next time it will be a sentence in the past.
I know it will come
And all of my strengths are drawn from that.

December 31, 1987

Your Pain

The pain you feel
Is also my pain.
I cannot bear to see your sadness
Yet I am unable to comfort you as I wish I might.
It was years ago I shared these feelings
And the event shall never leave my heart.
You can't help but wonder
What the creation may have been.
Trust me, just think of yourself.
It keeps the mind sane and the body complete.
I love you. I am here for you.
God I wish I could let you know
How I share your pain.

April 13, 1988

In My Mind

I talk to you all the time.
Yet I am mute when we are alone.

I am with you all the time.
But not how I may desire.

I always listen to you,
But you never speak the words I long to hear

We never touch,
But I crave the electricity of your closeness

I think of you always,
But my thoughts only imprison my actions.

You act like these words could be your own,
However I think you know my feelings
And only torture me with your presence.

For now, I'll just keep things in my mind
And trust you cannot read it.

May 6, 1988

To Capture the Moment

I could not believe the height to which I soared.
I didn't know the passion in my soul.
It was strangely ironic,
How reality presented itself like the dream.
Only the sense of incompleteness
Separated us from a special kind of bond.

I was grateful for the chance to experience such release
And yet amazed at the discipline of restraint.

This won't be relived.
It simply can't.
Yet I shall never forget my pursuit…

To capture the moment.

May 13, 1988

Advice

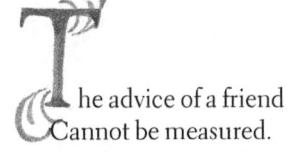

The advice of a friend
Cannot be measured.

Drawing from one's experience
Saves pain and unrest.

But you have to learn to
Stop hearing
And begin to listen.

When something begins to make sense
You cannot deny the inevitable any longer.

In this case it is time to say goodbye
Before too many bridges are burned.

Dear friend, thanks for your words,
I shall always be grateful.

July 18, 1988

Lightning

The lightning bolts have returned
Commiserate with your presence.
Ironically, it is my exterior displaying the calmness of the eye.
But inside winds are swirling,
Thunder is clapping and raindrops are beating.
You seem to return once a year,
And it takes that long for these daily thoughts to leave.
To see you every day would be unthinkable.
To see you not at all, unbearable.
I am grateful for the lightning you cause.
It lets me remember I am alive,
Alive for the purpose of one day being a part of your life.

August 2, 1988

Dragon's Jaws

The jaws of the dragon beckon my approach.
The distance seems so small.
Yet as my mind ignores its surroundings
The fire ahead captures all my attention.
This long-absent sense seems at odds
With the boundless growth of realism
That pervades my pores
And makes me yearn to be swallowed.
I am whole in body.
Yet empty of substance.

October 5, 1988

The Building Which Destroys

I suppose elation should occupy my days.
But this has had to make way for despair.
All of life's responsibilities keep piling on my shoulders.
I can carry no more and am in danger of collapse.

I must constantly drive myself to address the smallest of tasks.
My mind has been squeezed into exhaustion.

Discussion will not change these words.
Only one item controls this bullied spirit.
Yet strangely, upon reflection,
I feel so grateful,
For at least the opportunity of having lived.

January 26, 1989

Where to Turn?

As the days turn into weeks
And weeks into months
I react as a passerby,
Curious of what those days deliver
But apathetic as to what they offer.

As the clock turns and turns
I know not where to turn.
I simply observe the events shaping my life
Doing what should be done
Leaving no room for independent desires.

But sadly enough for the first time in my life
If someone said "Make a wish"
I couldn't.
I have even lost track of my dreams.
I have become a shell
Awaiting the inevitable crack,
But unable to defend against it.

February 1, 1989

My Search

The grip of fear is relentless,
Even as I scale the heights of the unimagined.
I am torn between pragmatism and frivolity
As this bounty looms within reach.

Patience has been its own reward,
But the material world cannot escape good fortune.
I should be elated as these events unfold.
Perhaps I am beyond the escape of sorrow.

As I continue to seek what may bring me some joy
It is obvious recent events
Has not put an end to my search.

April 19, 1989

Another Day

I have never felt so low.

As I learn, all I do know is the frustration of unhappiness
Is unrelenting and all encompassing.
Who can I share my burden with?
Who indeed?

The uncertainty of my self-composure and
Health of mind only increase my inner tension.
There is so much that must be done
And I wish to participate in none of it.

I know I have to,
But I cannot do it much longer.

The only achievements are small ones.
But they are not for me.
The sanity which binds is beyond that of clay
As I have managed to survive another day.

May 26, 1989

Apathy

The burning extremes of desire and reality
Have taken their toll.

I spend all of my time in consideration
Of what I don't want
Rather than reflecting on what I do.

I have been unclear regarding wants,
But those I don't pound my brain
And weaken walls already in collapse
From what bludgeons all—

Apathy.

June 1, 1989

Hmmm

I am reaching the end of my rope
Which was frighteningly short to begin with.
As I dangle in the breeze
Life's ebb and flow continues.

I can find no motive or strength to climb,
For it takes such power to simply hang on.
It shouldn't.
But it does.
I can't.
So I won't.

As I observe my destiny
It does not seem far away.

As the grip loosens,
The soul relaxes,
The mind indulges.

A calmness prevails.

Hmmm.

June 26, 1989

How Bad Could it Be?

This paper allows no description of you.
The words lie buried deep in my mind and heart
Yearning for the opportunity to be voiced
Yet aware that they may not.

Your presence spurns the process of imagination
And reality, as usual, maintains its relentless grip.
        Then you brush my arm and it sears!
And when you speak, I hang on every syllable.

I always have a smile for you.
God, I can't stand it
Knowing circumstances remain
Unchallenged by my reticence.

Fear of the greener grass
Contributes to inaction, but you know
I once said how bad could it be?
Before I created this mountain of misery.

Perhaps, if repeated, fate shall deliver
Me you
And provide the strength to deal with the situation.

How bad could it be?
How bad indeed.

October 6, 1989

Losing It

I laugh at myself so much of the time,
As I spit out my thoughts which don't ever rhyme.
All wrapped up in the life I lead
With failure to seek the things I need.

It's silly to indulge and to brood
When a turn of events may often include
A smile, a nudge to bring laughter again
But words must be spoken for comfort…and then

Life may go on with meaning and vigour
Feeling better of self but who'd ever figure
That happiness looms so far out of reach, not so true
It could all be reached by saying I want you.

What happens then could be victory or loss
As family, home and behaviour I toss
Out the window of prison to explore just a bit.
What tripe and nonsense,

       I'm losing it.

October 6, 1989

Motivation

I have never been so motivated
To pursue the pointless.

I have never so greatly anticipated
What shall not occur.

I cannot even look at your now,
But see you day after day.

This is tearing me apart
While attempts lie dormant.

I literally cannot get you off my mind.
This is not euphoric,
It is fear inducing.

I don't know why.
What worries me is I am so motivated to discover.

October 6, 1989

Longing

I long to speak my mind,
But responsibility leaves me mute.
I long to see you always,
But reality blinds my desires.

I long to touch your silken skin,
But my limbs heed other calls.
I wish to walk with you forever,
But these feet of clay cannot deliver.

I long to be with you as one,
But reticence maintains the divide.
I need to hear your approval,
But deaf ears would lend control.

All of our senses could deliver such wonder
And nothing need change…

Feel as I do.

We would not love them any less you know.

October 11, 1989

Serious

I tremble when you enter my thoughts.
Desire rises and falls,
But not this time.
It has yet to reach its peak.

Why you?

I cannot yet, offer words.

The summit of desire must wait
As the pursuit of its tip lies in repose
Coupled with my diligent retreat.

You enjoy the arduous ascent,
But this murderous climb
Shall not bring your head from the clouds.

I must reach you soon,
Before I slip down to Earth
And miss the chance to explain how serious I am.

October 11, 1989

Bang

This darkened tunnel
Has no light at its end,
But hope is not darkened by
Its imminent squeeze.

It triggers the imagination.
Yet this handle provides
The only way to get a handle on things.

The sight above destiny
Points to my end.
And the chamber awaits
My slumping existence.

As my grip tightens
I smile with eyes that sliver
And laugh at the method
I employ to deliver.

Yeah, I got a real bang out of life.

November 24, 1989

This is It

This is it.
The moment I have waited a lifetime for.
It's not bells and whistles
Or marching bands.

It's a presence,
All consuming and overpowering.
A single focus,
A mind and soul reeling experience.

It feels so personal and individual
The glory of which I am at loss to express.
But the world should know what I may not proclaim.

This is impossible to describe
With any other word
Than love.

At last my emotions are complete.
Oh how it tortures me I cannot share this with you.

December 21, 1989

Deliverance

Life has returned this body and spirit
To the form once unobtainable and the unsought.
But this is the way it is in matters of the heart.
It was meant to be discovered, not denied.

The path I have chosen is the logical one.
So what else is new?
Perhaps nothing has changed after all,
Only my outlook and inner sense of being.

Fate should deliver as it always has,
Good and bad.
A commitment to patience surpasses the immediate.

I'll be there when I'm needed,
As temporary as it may be.
But the permanence of heart shall be endorsed,
And then I'll decide

To control my own fate,
Or let destiny wield its awesome might.

December 28, 1989

Seasons

The last few weeks, though short,
Encompass a year of seasons.

The spring of hope,
      Anticipation and budding emotions.

Followed by…

Summer's heat,
      Enjoyment and burning optimism.

Followed by…

The fall of expectation,
      Dulling surroundings
      And awareness of the end.

Followed by…

Winter's crisp reality,
      Frozen efforts
      And snow-covered dreams.

Yet it does not end here.

For spring always follows winter.

January 4, 1990

Then and Now

Why could I write so freely
Of what I failed to understand.
The empty words which the past has scripted
Now have meaning and depth.

As I pour over them, they take on a new life.
Others inspired them,
But for you they exist.

I had written in hope of love I now know.
How can I be muted by the present
While volumes of history were devoid of feeling.

The words and I show new life,
A life you have granted by allowing me to love.

Should we never meet again
I shall be eternally in your debt.

January 17, 1990

Missing You

It seems an eternity since I last caught your smile
And enjoyed your company.

It seems forever since I smelled your hair
And its utopian aroma.

It seems so long since we leaned on each other
While walking down the hall.

It seems so distant since your fiery glance
Has emblazoned my soul
And the inner words brought a smile.

I miss these things.

I miss your beauty most of all,
And I miss the opportunity of being there
To remind you of my love.

The small things always bring you back.
It's so difficult for me…
When the tickle of any sense
Reminds me of you.

January 17, 1990

Enough is Enough

It's beating against a wall, I say
For reality maintains my head.
But I'm attempting to catch a butterfly
And this loving verse does spread.

From here to there in line upon line
While accomplishing nothing per se.
Give one's self a break and spare the time,
Do what you must the proper way.

Fear not lack of change and spare the rage.
A routine does suffice over time.
A goal of uniting must first disengage
And result in that so sublime.

This can't carry on much longer you know.
Come back to the ground that's so rough,
Spare all concerned and forget the show,
Realizing enough is enough.

January 17, 1990

Say When

I must be silent for now,
Should all chance be forestalled.

I know what must be done
And tell only myself.

These three monkeys show the way.
And serve to remind of the status quo.

It shall not be when I say,
But when you say when.

January 17, 1990

All I Need to Say

As my head swims,
From the myriad of words I wish to say,
My heart fails to cease sensing them.

I reel with repent when I do mutter forth.

I cannot do justice to my feelings with words.

It's as difficult to say as it is simple to feel.

I don't want or expect anything from you.

I know you.

That's all I need to say.

January 23, 1990

Blazing Eyes

Those blazing eyes
Which watch me depart
Set my soul on fire.

It's that look,
Which fills my heart,
Which reveals so little,
Yet says so much.

It says, be patient,
It says there's hope,
It says, someday,
It says, I feel, but cannot say.

When that look is gone
The world is benign.

One day those blazing eyes
Shall say,
Right now!
You may be mine.

February 9, 1990

Grief

This dampened "should"
Cannot provide answers,
Only strength.

This instrument of voice
Cannot say the right words,
Only utter them.

This trembling hand
Cannot lead you away.
It can only reach out.

These burning ears
Cannot bear your words of sadness,
They can only listen.

These caring eyes
Cannot reveal the pools of despair,
They can only observe.

Is it enough my body and soul
Ache as they share your despair?

No, because I may not be there
To deliver you from grief.

February 9, 1990

Yesterday's Pain

Allows for today's understanding,
While experience performs its soothing.

My body and soul twinge just a little
At the thought of never gaining your all.

I cannot pursue what lies beyond hope,
When I know it's a lark to you
And an all-consuming passion for me.

The divide must be so obvious.

I see and feel it,
But still choose to ignore reality's pull.

I'm deep in the knowledge of nothing to gain.
So I must retreat to the comfort of…

Yesterday's pain.

February 12, 1990

All by Myself

There are some conversations
You must have with only yourself.

Some big decisions are close at hand.
Yet counsel, once sought, may not be implored.

Instincts so long pushed aside
Must be followed and lived with.

I cannot deny my own direction forever
When inside myself, I know the course.

One cannot look back before going ahead.
This is my life.
And the worst that may happen is,

I'm all by myself.

Yet isn't that what I have wanted all along?

February 12, 1990

The Kiss of Change

"What a difference a kiss makes,"
So you once said.
As my mind raced with replies
I maintained stony silence,
For fear of altering my tack.

It has changed the level of confidence,
It has changed the scope of relationship,
It has forged a bond, however small.

It has changed the focus of the past,
And has changed the desires of the future.

It has significance for many reasons.
Although that kiss may not have changed the world,

      It certainly has changed mine.

February 21, 1990

Sixth Sense

What I see I may never have.
What I hear can never be understood.
What I feel can never be realized.
What I say changes nothing.
What I taste is defeat.
Only a sixth-sense can negate all others
And deliver what I need.

February 22, 1990

Surrender

Mind versus heart.

It has always been no contest,
For thought always reigns over emotion.

I constantly battle now
In the war of mind and soul.

I know how it is going to be.
To retreat is the logical tack.
But this relentless heart pulls me forward.

Strength lies in compartments and dogma.
But the heart tears down walls,
And the heart alters the truth.

I may as well give up and proceed
With an unconditional surrender to the heart.

March 9, 1990

What Are You Thinking?

I need to know,
Since you say so little,
Let nothing show.

I may have been wrong
About a kiss like that.
The odd little glance,
Some whimsical chat.

But hope's all I have
To stop from sinking.
Yet to float
I must know what you're thinking.

March 13, 1990

The Essence of Change

The essence of change
Is what makes life so enjoyable.

A stagnant existence
Creates nothing to feed our desires.

As I observe my emotions,
It' like watching someone else.

It all seems so pointless,
But then I didn't ask for this.

I suppose if we create newness
Things have already been accepted.

But when you think about it,
Isn't acceptance the essence of change?

March 16, 1990

The Building of Trust

I had never given trust much thought.
I either trusted someone or not,
And considered little one's trust in me.

It has become a challenge to gain yours.
As we spar with exchanges of knowledge
To try and prove our willingness to confide.

Strange for something established
Without question
That shared afternoon.

Secrets guard the pillars of trust.

However, trust does not mean full disclosure.
Trust is a willingness to confide without fear of release.
Trust is being unafraid to be yourself.

It's too late to question loyalties.
The foundations have already been laid

For the building of trust.

March 16, 1990

Influence

As I consider all that has influenced my life —
Parents, song, the written word and emotion —
One always seems to drive harder than the others
At various times.

A child's world reflects the call of elders.
       He cannot deny direction.
Youth rebels to anthems of word and music.
       And cannot deny their meanings.
But the mature individual
       Cannot deny the heart.

As the past has an influence on us all,
It is the present which carries the burden of feelings.

Past events may have become a blur.
Present ones shall one day be the same.
So, my love for you,
Which for now
Cannot be denied,
Simply must be forgotten
Because…
       I simply can't deal with its influence.

March 20, 1990

The Word (I)

Just give me the word
And I'm out of your life.
As my desire for you grows
I'm curious of the ripple effect.

The wandering mind.
The denial of responsibility.
All else becoming a lesser priority.

But thankfully
I have become too bothersome.
Things are more trouble than they are worth.
Yet I need to know for certain.

For once a bad thought crosses your mind,
It is already too late.
There are no need for words.

Always know I am only a sigh away.

March 22, 1990

Anticipation

The waiting and anticipation
Build to a pitch
As my upward glance goes unrewarded.

Then the mirror transforms
Into the fairest of portraits.

Its reflection offers the image
Of life's passion and desire.

At last the opportunity to engage
In the ritual of verbal parry and thrust.

I think the anticipation
Is the best part.
And I once read
Anticipation is already nine tenths of the act itself.

April 20, 1990

Friends

All I want to do is cry out I love you!
In the hope it will change your heart's direction.

But my promise of long-term friendship
Strains my desires and leaves me in silence.

It won't be easy, yet I never break a promise.

But if that's what you want,

I love you so much

I can't deny your wish…

To be friends.

April 30, 1990

What's Wrong?

It burns away at me.
It's constant and unabating,
Never leaving my thoughts,
And allowing for thoughts of nothing else.

I can't let this get to me.
You have nothing to gain
By making me feel this way,
And you refuse to discuss it.

I shall not pursue it specifically
Or anything generally.
Enough is wrong right now without this.

I guess this is it.
Words won't cure anything.
All has been lost.
But I don't know why.

And I wish I didn't care.

May 23, 1990

Out of My Mind

You have become an obsession.

I feared this may happen,
But it has been impossible to avoid.

I cannot bear being alone,
Because all I think of is you.

Every station plays reminders of you.
Every dream is filled with you.

The situation has gotten out of hand
So the solution is to get you out of my mind.

June 1, 1990

My World

I'm doing my best to block you out,
But the mind can only work so hard.
There are times when you drift away,

Just ever so.

Then a sound, sight or smell,
Brings you right back,

Just ever so.

It's all I can do to ignore the phone,
But how can I
When it puts me in touch
With my world…

The one that revolves around you.

June 7, 1990

A Song for You

I keep wishing I could write a song for you
It's composer's thoughts I long to share,
But the words must be my own and must be true
When I sing it strong and proud you must be there.

The lyrics tell a story of love in vain
Yet the words reach out from my heart to yours,
Every thought of you and all my inner pain
Give me the words to open up your doors.

The notes are sweeter than the sweetest flower
Every strum and beat begs to be for you.
All the sound lives for your ears which could deliver
My notes of love and feelings ever true.

The verses tell of how your beauty reigns
And your sparkling wit and girlish smile,
Of your eyes that burn till nothing else remains
And my love for you which cannot seek denial.

The chorus would repeat my love for you
Say again my devotion cannot fail.
It tells of loving feelings as they grew
And grants me prose to tell this loving tale.

I live for you
And what I hope to be.
It's all on your small shoulders,
Say "I love you" and the words would set me free.
This love I have is all there is to me.
And nothing takes the place of seeing you there.
All I think of is togetherness and see,
How my life's complete without a single care.

Now this chorus shall repeat my love for you.
Tell again how my devotion cannot fail.
Tell of these loving feelings as they grew.
And gives me words to tell this loving tale.

June 12, 1990

Just as Well

I've discovered the error of my ways.
You see, I played with an open hand,
And I played all my cards up front,
Forgetting you shouldn't in pursuit of dreams.

I've eliminated the chase, the mystery,
And all that drives the curious.
It has been too long since I have played the game.
The rules don't change and certainly not the approach.

It's time to withdraw.
There is nothing left up my sleeve.
The deck has diminished.
More than likely it was stacked
Against me from the beginning.

However, it may be I'll never know.

And perhaps it's just as well.

June 15, 1990

Some Space

You don't seem yourself right now.
But perhaps it is I who has changed.
I am too concerned with what you think and feel,
As the pressure builds,
Only to be moving further away.

I must give up.

Why can't I go with my instincts?
They got me this far with you.
Now they must draw me away.

Things must be taken at face value.

It seems you need some space.
I just want everything to be all right,
Yet know they shall not.

June 15, 1990

In Your Eyes

In your eyes
I see things clearly,
perhaps for the first time.

This has brewed a strange mix
of elation and devastation.
The first based on love, hope and desire.
The latter, the effects of serious pursuit.

I've almost taken pride in my apathy.
Yet reckless pursuit and damn the consequences
just isn't me.

I have grown less patient, for the most part,
which is truly an unfortunate end.
But I am showing signs of life
for the first time in my life.

As my wonderment builds
I maintain this disguise
and yearn for the next chance
to reflect…

in your eyes.

July 10, 1990

This Day in Your Life

At last! You sigh
as the vows end
and reality sets in.
Such celebration cannot end.
It's all so wonderful,
        isn't it?

The sharing of souls,
the joining of hearts,
the single-mindedness of purpose.

I hope these do not give way
to the splitting of hairs,
the division of emotions,
the emergence of self.

All wishes are sincere and gracious,
as life together should be,
        shouldn't it?

The fantasy shall live,
for endurance is innate.

And only the good should be considered
on…

This day in your life.

August 9, 1990

Summit

There is no summit
which measures the height of my love for you.

These mountainous feelings
have peaked when the scale is behind me,
but no flag could be set.

It has been a defeat.
As one must always bear in mind,
there is no victory in climbing,

only conquering.

August 25, 1990

The Power of Words

Words of promise for one
are words of demise for another.

It all sounds so wonderful,
but it tears at my soul,
while you give yours to another.

"I do," said you
and the earth split, swallowing my existence,
and ridding me of pain
created by the power of words.

"I will," hear I
as oblivion is all that remains.
These words should be for my ears
so the embodiment of all that has worth
could be discovered, explored and absorbed.

As it ended
so too did everything else,
creating only a void.
How can I go on
when it has all been ended…

By the power of words.

August 25, 1990

One Event

Never has one event
filled me with such contradiction.
The last thing I want is for this to occur
yet it must for the status quo.

I have grown more depressed
as the days pass.
They shall come and go.
The sun will rise tomorrow.
But it just won't shine as bright.

What shall I do now?
The game is over before it began.
Best to fade away, slowly
and return to self, quickly.

But why did this have to happen now
when I am discovering who I am,
and realizing who, and what, I need
knowing these can't ever be realized?

All because of one event.

August 26, 1990

The Other Side

The opaque spheres
blur a vision of life itself.

I'm unable to quite see through
yet know what's on the other side anyway.

This constant straining to see something
other than the obvious
defeats my bid to carry on.

But, by not going ahead
I can sit back and reflect.

Perhaps this is not the time for clarity
since the numbness sustained
is as pleasant
as what's on the other side,
is not.

August 26, 1990

Today

All is not lost!

Because you still have that look.
Your silence remains,
but it's still there,
some small desire, I know it.

Fate shall have us along one day
and words will be shared
and actions will be real.

Whether brief or extended,
this gift of time shall put doubts to rest.

Just knowing how you feel
would be enough for contentment
        as long as life
        or pain
        as sharp as any soul could endure.

We're not finished yet.
We have not even begun.
It is this thought that keeps me together
during times when we are apart.

October 5, 1990

Back in Touch

Life has become a challenge of late
as I rid myself of all that harms me.

No more inhalation, consumption
and certainly no more dreams.

When faced with the ultimate in giving up,
perhaps deleting all of life's little pleasures
may just put me back in touch with the things that really matter
or at least, used to.

So we'll be in touch.
At least one day we'll talk.

October 15, 1990

The Note

There were just too many questions
And simply not enough patience
To find the answers.

October 19, 1990

Looking Ahead

Since I seem to be looking ahead
I have begun to realize what it takes
to get back to myself.

And as simply as I can put it:

Nobody is worth discovering
while it's me I'm losing.

October 19, 1990

At Peace (II)

At last I am at peace with myself
having chosen a path
convinced its direction is true.

This path is straight, consistent
and predicable, so as not to lose my way
and cause diversions,
unhealthy for the heart and soul.

This path provides answers and has let me know
there comes a time for everything
but the time is not now.
There comes a time when you want to take,
`cause giving is not enough.

It helps me be honest with myself
while recognizing my boundaries and limitations.

On this path,
prayers are not always answered,
hearts are not always endorsed,
minds are not always clear.

However, this path provides
      direction,
      stability,
      and release
back to who I was.

Perhaps this path stems from a circle.
If so, another trip around shall not find me
'cause for the first time, in a long time,

      I'm at peace.

October 31, 1990

Looking Back

I often wonder
when looking back on our lives
is it more important
to have led a happy one
or a responsible one?

I fear I'm incapable of both.

November 13, 1990

What to Do?

These highs and lows
are drifting to the latter,
as things add up
it really doesn't matter.

Concern for freedom
and time alone
but dreams gone by,
a sigh, a moan.

So carry on,
the choices are few.
God give me the answers
on what to do.

November 14, 1990

A Year Ago Today

A year ago today
our voices sang as one,
our minds thought alike,
our eyes met,
our arms reached out,
our bodies entwined,
our lips explored,
our fate was assured…

Or so I thought.

It was a day
when dreams began,
        only to end.
When hope prevailed,
        only to fade.
When a soul beckoned,
        only to die.

And I learned,
when you want something
infinitely more than someone else,
it shall only remain a desire,
never becoming a reality.

If only I had known that,
a year ago today.

December 21, 1990

Failure

A year ago today
my world expanded
and as I ventured into new emotional territory
I failed in the quest which my heart sent me on.

Yet, on the way
I learned some things about myself,
good and bad.
But what difference does it make?
The fact is I failed.

Unfortunately I learned
failure did not beget success,
it simply endorsed
the mediocrity of my current existence.

December 21, 1990

Anyone

I gave a year and held nothing back.
With the written word I penned unending love.
With my speech I confirmed my devotion.
With my actions I showed my dedication.
With my heart and soul I made my pledge.
And all you had to say was,
    It could have been anyone.
I died with those words.
But I should also bid thanks,
for now I stop playing the fool.

February 8, 1991

As Simple as That

The sense of loss I feel
escapes description.
I have brought it upon myself no doubt
and it is what I wanted
        but just not this way.

What is more precious
than any of the world's offerings is gone.

I didn't have the patience I professed.
Yet I simply can't take the waiting.
    I simply can't worry about what I say.
    I simply can't worry about the way I look.
    I simply can't take my mind always being full of her.

I am not very good at being in love.

It's as simple as that.

April 25, 1991

The Wound of Time

The day passed without a thought
and has settled into obscurity
joining every other passion I have confronted.

How could this of all celebrations go unnoticed
while the calendar guides me to the past,
a past of euphoria and bliss and life,
a past of honesty with you
and more importantly with myself.

But if time heals all wounds
this canyon of lust splits my heart
and a millennium shall only deepen it.
For life simply flows through.
And as life remains empty
so does this divide,
created by reality meeting desire
and hope versus monotony.

These wishful thoughts
and beckoning heart
help close the gap.
Yet the heart shall not be whole
till our hands join,
our minds share a dream,
our hearts beat as one,
and our souls span the abyss.

December 23, 1991

One Day You Awaken

After years of saying "no" and "be quiet"
and "stop" and "be careful"
one day you awaken
and you hope
they aren't into drugs,
their abstinence is true,
their lungs are free,
they think behind the wheel,
and their virtue is intact.

I guess the worry of the past
becomes worry for their future
while the present influences
were shaped and are shaping
a soul of grace and caring and pride.

So one day you awaken
with a smile
from your efforts
and their results
and you don't worry
for you have not been forsaken

when one day you awaken.

December 23, 1991

In Case You've Forgotten

I still love you,
        you know.
In case you've forgotten.

As the years pass by
I find myself as enchanted as ever
and the spell you once cast, still remains,
        you know.
In case you've forgotten.

My heart still explodes at the sight of you
And reveals those feelings denied,
but never buried.
And love's light beams from every pore,
        you know.
In case you've forgotten.

I am not around as much
as distance provides peace of mind.
But my heart still beats,
        you know.
In case you've forgotten.

I still marvel at it all.
What I should avoid.
But I should not be avoided,
`cause I'm still here,
        you know.
In case you've forgotten.

December 23, 1992

A Time

It is that time of year.
A time of caring,
when I care so little.
A time of giving,
when I wish to take.
A time of sharing,
when I want something, anything, just for myself.
A time of reflection,
when I want to forget.
A time of loving,
when I have none in my heart.
A time of peace,
as the internal battles rage on.
A time like any other,
for all of these things are perpetuated
by knowing it is appropriate
to care, to give, to share, to love.

I just can't do it much longer.

December 24, 1992

III

Moments

Nine years ago today my life changed.
I did not know it then.
We rarely recognize
The moments that dictate a lifetime.
The moments that force one's hand.
The moments that leave no recourse.
The moments that shape the future.

I have lived a few of these moments
And I am living with the results.
What's common in all is I have never chosen them.
I have had no bearing on the outcome,
Only the start.

Fate?

Perhaps.

Destiny?

Indeed.

I cannot cherish the thought
Of how these moments have
Caused me to languish among the masses
While reflecting at this moment.

September 20, 1994

The Cure

Ten years ago today
I wrote of a cure
that has yet to deliver.

Why don't I care about anything I have?
Anything!

I have nothing:
No peace.
No sanity.
No contentment.
No direction.
And certainly no cure.

As we build a life,
we build responsibilities
that become bigger than life.

In retrospect, ten years ago seemed so simple
compared with today.
God knows what I am creating for the next ten years.

This momentum must stop.
But it is bigger than me.
Bigger than the advice I can seek.
Bigger than the dollar can buy.
Bigger than the comfort of God.

But not as big as the cure.

September 20, 1994

Unrelenting

It's been a long time since I felt this way
but a millisecond of consideration
makes me realize nothing has changed in the past decade.
It is a long time to experience such sadness.
Not only have I lost my dreams,
I have lost my sense of reality.

You can only drift for so long.
Well, for now I plot these entries,
knowing one day I shall look back and shrug.

The reality is another decade shall pass.
Unchanged…
Unchecked…
Unrealized…
But worst of all…

Unrelenting.

September 24, 1994

Special

If it were all to end today
There would be a smile on my face.
Why?

Because I know there was a moment,
A brief moment, when your only thought
In the world was me.

And a brief moment when my only thought
In the world was you.

It was a lifetime ago,
But it was there
And it was real
And it was special…
Very special.

December 24, 1994

Time to Row

I saw myself so clearly the other day.
I was in a lifeboat
drifting…drifting
confident, somewhere over the horizon
a rescue lay imminent.

Lo, it was not to be
nor shall it.
For if I'm drifting…drifting
that is all I shall do.

But I began to paddle
just a little.
It took place in my mind
but the momentum was undeniable.

Briefly, I thought I saw something.
And I did.
I saw control.
I saw direction.
I saw a mountain's peak.

As I paddled in the peak's direction
there was hope
for little by little,
stroke by stroke,
I was gaining control.

It felt good and feels good.
The peak waits,
the summit is in view
and the oar is in the water.

November 10, 1995

Lifetimes

It seems like a lifetime
since the opportunity presented itself.

I am not sure how it is going,
but it's going.

The sharing of our past is something
to build a future on.
This is a beginning of sorts
but this will take the whole nine yards
…an inch at a time.

If this takes another lifetime
then so be it.
The problem is I am running out of lifetimes
so I shall have to make the most of this one.

October 7, 1996

Alone

When I heard you were alone
I knew I no longer would be.

I can remember the charge,
the excitement,
and the anticipation
when I got the news.

However, the courage lay dormant for a time.
It seems overcoming shyness does not come easy.

But here we are
and where that is, I am not certain.

At least we are not alone,
for now…

November 2, 1996

Sparks

I was sitting in the dark today,
both literally and metaphorically
considering how protective that can be.

As I allowed my thoughts to wander,
I began to wonder.

When you live in the shadow of reality,
the sun never burns.
Besides, that was the plan.

I was supposed to be taking my time.

If I had any self-confidence before today
it certainly went up in flames.
I always thought you needed sparks to start a flame.

I am somewhat perplexed by my reaction to today's events.
There wasn't any emotional investment here.
It seems I am a little more fragile than I thought.

The fat lady is already on her way to the next gig.
Her song oh so familiar to me.

So it's back to the original plan
With no detours or distractions.
The cage awaits once again.

So I can regroup, recoup
And most of all regret
That there weren't any sparks.

November 3, 1996

Instincts

Finally I went with my instincts.
It hurt a little, well, a lot.
But they were right,
and being right
saves time, energy and pain.
The reason we have instinct
is to warn, to avoid and to release.
This is not head-over-heart nonsense,
this is gut.
I did it.
Yes I did.

November 3, 1996

Plus ça change

I'm surprised at my lack of focus at the moment
since all of the plans required an abundance.
My mind is on overdrive
as my goals fade to black.
How did I get off course?

As I make things easy for someone else
the harder things become for me.
What sense does that make?

Speaking of sense,
I did the sensible thing yet again.

They say what comes around goes around.
Unfortunately as it comes around,
I let it pass me by,
or I don't recognize it's on its way,
or perhaps it's just never for me.

As I drive this plan
I have to pick up the pace
or I will never reach my destination.
But I do not know where it is,
what it is,
or how to get there.

I should take some comfort
on this familiar road.

Plus ça change…

November 4, 1996

Signals

Hot   Cold
Off   On
In   Out
Up   Down
Near   Far
Yes   No   Maybe

God…if mixed signals are blessings
this women is a saint.

December 5, 1996

Upstream

I've gone from drifting
to getting the drift.

Now, too tired to keep
paddling upstream,
I'm back to shore for supplies.

My arms are weary,
my legs are weak,
and my spirit is broken.

The river of experience
is a winding one
with obstacles to avoid
and silent turns to negotiate.

The oar of confidence has snapped
but a replacement can be found I trust
for the journey has only begun.

I have avoided the falls for now.
It was a tributary lending the insight.

I shall portage to Hope,
build a new base camp
and claim my stake
or be claimed.

I'll be okay.
As long as I stay upstream.

December 5, 1996

The Real Thing

If I only knew what you were looking for.
Perhaps I do—
It is the real thing.
But what is it?

It's about all the assets I fail to possess:
Charm, age, class, dignity and above all a presence.

It struck like lightning last night
And so I'm running for cover.

If only I carried myself a little better,
Had a little more mileage than years,
And the stature in place.

Well, at least I have the grace to bail out,
The maturity to recognize,
And the presence of mind.

I shall always have these and more.
Unfortunately, I will never
Be in possession of…
"The real thing."

December 5, 1996

Check-Out Time

What I am trying to capture
Is not the moment this time.
It's forever.

The process stretches out minute by minute,
Conversation by conversation,
Inch by inch.

If there was at least something within reach
ever-present optimism would kick in.

But illusive ill describes the verdict
And jury has yet to be chosen
Let alone its verdict.

No contest can best describe
The reality and all of its derivatives
And the result ignites the internal
Checks and balances

For it is time to check out.
Someone else needs the room.
But it is okay,
Because I didn't bring any bags
And I didn't even disturb the sheets.
No, I didn't even disturb the sheets.

December 5, 1996

Just Another Day

I understand your sadness,
But I am unable to relate to it as you do.

Bear in mind
It is only the calendar
Offering this day any significance.

It was a day of beginning,
I shall grant you that.
And I suppose a day to reminisce.

But what began long ago,
Has run its course.

It may no longer serve as a beginning,
It may only represent a passage.

So for now and forever…
It is just another day.

December 16, 1996

Yours

You shall never know
What you have done for me
In such a brief period of time.

You have shown me caring and excitement,
Laughter and passion.

You are guiding me back to the world
And for that it is ours to share,
And for that I am grateful,
And for that I am yours.
And for that…

December 17, 1996

The Challenge

There is something in your eyes
Which captivates my imagination
And rewards me with a crinkle
From time to time.

I also see some pain,
Which lingers
And motivates me to eliminate
All that could cause any sadness.

But the sparkle
Which ignites such joy
And reels in my heart
Allows you some freedom for the moment.

The challenge is to stretch
The moment to a lifetime.

December 18, 1996

Attitude

I own the world right now
And it does not take riches
To achieve this status.
It takes attitude and passion.

And as these things return
I begin to reflect on all the possibilities
The future shall lend.

It feels so good to feel good
So I'll take this ride for as long as it goes
Knowing when you're on top
It is not forever,
But I don't care.

And for a change, that's not apathy talking,
It's attitude.

December 19, 1996

Numbness

Nothing could have prepared me for today.
It was written all over your face.
Your upward glance was your betrayal
As it froze my mind and spirit.

All of my life I've heard
Winners and losers state
It might sink in tomorrow,
Thinking what a silly response.

I now know of what they speak,
For the moment offers nothing
But a numbness,
Nothing but a void,
Nothing as it runs so deep.

I cannot imagine what
Tomorrow's thoughts may bring.
For now I am grateful for the numbness
And the protection it offers
From the moment,
From the prospect,
From today.

December 29, 1996

Nothing

I am afraid after today
I am either your friend or I am nothing.
The communication will not exactly be flowing
For an event of this nature provides no catalyst.
I need you to help me deal with this.
Strange, when I have never needed you before.
I wish I could just sleep and greet tomorrow
With an open mind
And a sense of conviction.

I am afraid I am gone.

I do not wish to be nothing,
However I deserve nothing more.

December 29, 1996

No Longer

The news filled me with a sense of joy
And validity.

Recall, if you will,
The purpose of my departure.
And what I could not sustain
Was ruled by apathy,
Controlled by indifference,
And monitored by disenchantment.

But you have already achieved
What I was not prepared to give
Simply because you didn't deserve it.

This state of lust you proclaim
And which you claimed at seventeen
Lends a smile
Because at least you cared for me once
And that can never be taken away.

Yet as the appropriate thought approaches
I swat it away like a bug too persistent
For my liking.
It has circled my being for a lifetime
And guided my unhappiness.

No longer do I live for you.
No longer do I act on your behalf.
No longer do I let you in.
And no longer do you control.

No longer…do you control.

December 29, 1996

Earth, Wind and Fire

When you are near
It's as if I'm surrounded
By desire, passion,
And a profound sense of purpose.

Your touch causes tremors
That would put Richter to shame
And shakes into place
A long forgotten will.

I have been akin to a dormant volcano,
A hurricane in repose,
An earthquake waiting to happen.

Though these may represent destruction
They truly deliver a sense of awe and power and wonder
Equalled only by the reality of being with you.

And as I reflect on these earthly intrigues
I cannot fail to desire your earthly delights.

But you have walls
Which these forces should defeat
But more importantly must respect.

This is not a race for shelter.
This is a journey of the senses
And as the walls crumble
Or perhaps lose their height

I can only marvel at the prospect.

January 1, 1997

The Journey

So, you wish to get to know me.
All right.
But I am afraid you'll run and hide.

There has been a darkness,
An elusiveness,
And an apathetic past.

I can show you
And I can tell you who I was

Then beg you to stay.
And beg you I do,
In joining me to discover who I am.

The journey began with you.

January 2, 1997

Finally

Today I wept.
I have tried for years
To offer a physical presence
To the innate sadness and despair.
But I think they are tears of joy.
Finally hope and dismay
Have met in the ring.
There was clearly a winner
And for a change I believe it was me.

January 2, 1997

Last Night

I'm trying to gather my thoughts.
They stretch from the attire to the action
Of last night.

It is all there:
The anticipation,
The feedback,
The guidance,
The communication,
The validation,
The selflessness,
The partnership.

I could not stop thinking of the expression
"You do not know what you've got till it's gone."
I disagree.
I can only say you do not know what you've
been missing till you've had it.

I want this to go on forever.

January 3, 1997

Why You

Here is what you offer the world,
As I see it anyway.

You are independent,
But you still need somebody.

You are intelligent,
Yet there is still so much to learn.

You portray a certain toughness,
But softness lurks inside.

You have courage,
But a little nudge never hurts.

You have class
And grace
And a smile…

Oh that smile!

And that's why you.

January 5, 1997

...And Then Some

I feel a little like a prospector hitting the motherlode.
I am looking around wondering if it is really true.
I can't spend it all because it will be gone.
Yet some must be spent because subsistence simply exists.
Timing is everything in the world of subtlety.

This new-found wealth must be managed well,
Handled with care,
And certainly observed wisely.

For now all the intentions are banked,
The rate of withdrawal to be determined
By this precious substance itself.

Like all precious gems
They must not be exploited, wasted or ignored.
They must be treated with pride, care and attention.

So that they last forever...
And then some.

January 13, 1997

The Last Night

As you lay across my chest,
I felt your heart beat
Emitting its pain
And asking for the pain's retreat.

I never wanted to leave your arms last night
Nor any night for that matter.
But I felt strangely unable to help.
I was there, but it wasn't enough.

I will always be there if you wish.
Hopefully to revel in your triumphs
And lift your spirits during tribulations.

But when it comes to seeing you in pain
I hope
It was the last night.

January 17, 1997

The Word (II)

I almost said it last night.
But I have always been reticent
In using the word,
For fear I may mean it.

And as the word signifies
Joy, passion and completeness.
It may also deliver
Trepidation, uncertainty and vulnerability.

As I ponder the direction in which we head,
It might confuse us both.
But it is there for me
Just waiting to be said.

January 17, 1997

Human

As you were all but apologizing for being human
I felt a surge of caring and love.
You became a whole person right in front of my eyes.
Sure, you were fragmented, vulnerable and weak
But my love for you became solid, protective and strong.
And as you lay in my arms,
My mind and soul soared
Knowing I was the one in whom you confided,
And I was the one in whom you placed your trust,
And I was the one you needed at that moment.
You may have thought you were taking
But I can't begin to describe what you gave.
You gave all of yourself to me
And not at the heights when it's easiest,
But at the lowest when it's the most difficult.
And there is nothing more human than that.

January 17, 1997

Helium

Loving you feels like helium
making me ever lighter,
lifting me…lifting me,

taking me to the stratosphere
where I witness the stars
reminding me of your eyes that sparkle,
observing the planets
which represent a distance from you
I could never contemplate.

And as gravity pulls me back to reality
I still love you

on the ground,
in the air
and especially in your arms.

       I love you.

January 20, 1997

Closure

I wish there was a world without closure.
It would imply all good things
Had not necessarily come to an end
Or bad things had not been created.

It is a time we break with the past
Guided by present contentment
And dreams of the future
Which may lend a hand
In grabbing the moment
While we release the years.

Yet why reopen
The wounds of time, words and behaviour
Just to sew them back up,
Mark them with a wrap
And send them on their way
Never to return.

That's why.
So as never to return.

January 23, 1997

Waiting

As I stare at the phone
And beg for my world to be unaltered,
A certain fear creeps in.
The seconds hang like fog
Blocking what I see as truth
But fail to accept.

It is so difficult to focus
As you spar with the past.

All of the insecurities
Float to the surface
And tough questions beg a response.

Can you love me as you did them?
Am I good enough for you?
Do I deserve your love?
Can I fulfill your dreams and expectations?

Of your response, I have no doubt,
And I only wish I could believe you
As I only wish I could believe in myself.

January 23, 1997

Not Because of Him

I know I have upset you and
I am in agony awaiting your forgiveness.

I'm always on the edge,
Praying there are no slip ups,
And demanding perfection.

I can't pass every test you throw at me.
I refuse to be haunted by your past
Because I have no control over
The effect it has had on you.

This is our life together
So judge it as ours
On its merits
And should I fail,
Let it be because of me
And not because of him.

January 29, 1997

On the Beach

For years I had but one desire:
To be alone.

Now I shudder at the thought.

Had I stayed with the plan
This sorrow would be nonexistent
Or at least delayed.

I put my toe in the sea of vulnerability
And was crushed by a rogue wave.

Even as I saw its approach
Every instinct was pleading I get out of the way.

But I stood my ground
And the ground has been washed away,
Along with my body and spirit and will.

Another visit to the beach is not forthcoming.

January 30, 1997

Wonder

For Emma-Lee

As I watch you grow,
It is with wonder and delight.
I love to share in the triumphs
You have enjoyed
And those which shall follow.
I am here to help during times of stress
And to answer the questions which
A growing life brings forward.
I have no expectations
Beyond hoping you are happy and complete
And that your efforts in any endeavour
Are your best.
I shall always love you
And be here for you
Because you bring me such happiness
And pride,
And wonder.

February 14, 1997

Words of Peace

As you quietly whispered your feelings,
Followed by my name
A contentment and delight enveloped me.

To be taken by sleep at that moment
Was to be at peace within
And all that surrounded me.

Your words fill my heart
And a sigh of relief leaves my spirit
Knowing you are so close,
Providing the safety and reassurance
That only love provides,

And I've spent a lifetime seeking.

March 11, 1997

Dried Flowers (II)

As I checked on your dried flowers
I couldn't help but relate
To the journey they had taken.

Their seeds were our meeting,
Their gift was our bond,
Their bloom was our love,
Their short life our togetherness,
Their inevitable death our destiny,
Their current state my memories,
Strangely pretty, yet dry and lifeless.

The life of a rose is so fragile,
As was ours.
There is no sorrow in that.
The rose knows it,
And so did I.

March 14, 1997

Holly

A close friend said I should fight for you,
This is what love is, she told me.
Keeping her was hard enough to do,
Getting her back is impossible for me.
I am not sure what I want.
I feel a sense of relief, I confess.
There are her rules that taunt
And when I break them what a mess.
I have a plan to follow,
To ignore it would be folly.
Best leave things alone
And simply miss my Holly.

March 14, 1997

Destiny

Destiny called us together
And as I cover my ears
This fails to block the continuing echo
Of life, love, our togetherness
We were meant to share.

I believe in this calling
As fate is powerful and undeniable.
However, what becomes of the course
Of action, direction, events
We were meant to share?

Your news has rocked my world
And strangely, I can only recall the good
Which made me stay,
Not the bad,
Which forced our separation.

Is it destiny ringing in my ears these days
Or solitude not offering what I expected?
How do I approach you with this dilemma
Of confusion, desire, need?

Yet I know this:
I miss you
And I love you
But I cannot be with you
Until destiny not only speaks
But acts.

April 10, 1997

This Torch

As you stirred, prompting my glance,
You personified an angel
Within reach, but as always, elusive.

As we exchanged greetings,
I melted
And grew a little closer to you.

I shall carry the image
Till it fades
As I will carry this torch
Till it no longer burns.

April 24, 1997

I Just Am

As the days slip by
And the memories of us get filtered,
I have begun to think of a future without you.
How long term were we anyway?

You look at life much differently than I,
And I promised to change for nobody.
I lost myself once before
And it shall never happen again.

I cannot share your intensity.
I cannot share nor understand your sense of drama.
I can only share your passion,
But for how long?

Our current status poses more questions
Than it provides answers.

So, it is time to move on.
I don't want to,
I just am.

May 6, 1997

No Idea

It is like a record playing
Over and over again in my head,
But these thoughts are not the speed of a record.
They represent the percentages of the driving forces
Behind my thoughts
Which shall evolve into actions:
Thirty-three percent of me shall wait,
Thirty-three percent of me says give fate a nudge,
Thirty-three percent of me says move on.

A hundred percent of me has no idea.

May 6, 1997

You're Back

So you're back,
The loose ends all tied,
The mind clear,
Spirit ascending,
The heart beckoning,
A hundred percent in the game.
I hope so.

Because all you have gone through
I have been sharing,
Albeit, on a smaller scale.
So we'll take this very slowly
Till you one day turn
Your back
Again.

May 20, 1997

Always Does

I can't imagine not having you in my life,
But as I am forced to think about it
It leads me back to my plan:
No encumbrances,
No deep thinking or dealings,
No risks, no rewards
But no downside either.

Hopefully the detachment process
Does the job,
But I somehow doubt it in your case.

You have touched my life…
Very deeply.

So the recovery process begins

Like a cut which now must heal,
Or a weight which must be lifted,
And a life which must go on.
As it always does,

Doesn't it?

May 27, 1997

What You Give

What you give me
Is beyond the written word
Or page.

And as I struggle in allowing
The pen to create its verse
I can only examine a presence,

One of caring, loving and giving
From you
Which provides me an inner smile
As wide as time
And as bright as the stars.

How you continue to give is beyond me and this pen
But you do.

I can only hope it inspires me in kind
To maintain some equilibrium.
I am grateful,
As I am becoming me
Because what you give

Is of yourself.
I love you.

August 7, 1997

Lake Holly

I am uncertain whether
The lake has inspired thoughts of you
Or you of the lake.

As I examine its silken surface
I am reminded of your skin
And as I contemplate its depths
This evokes thoughts of how deep
My love runs for you.

The peace it provides
Is matched only by
The peace of mind you grant
And the whisper of the wind
Tells me how I want you
And need you and love you.

While darkness lends
Itself to the moment
I still see its outline
Just as I see your face

Bringing me a smile
As I contemplate Four Mile.

It has become Lake Holly forever
Offering peace and tranquillity
And passion
Each time I look at it
And think of you.

I shall remember this moment for a lifetime
As I shall remember you.

August 7, 1997

Together...Forever

It was a sleepless night
As I pondered our lives
Together...forever
As one.

I lay with open eyes
And considered how you have opened my eyes
To the reality of commitment
And all that entails.

There should be no question
Given how I feel.
You always make sense no matter how
Intangible or lofty the topic.
And you provide such comfort with your love.

If it's right, it's right
Regardless of timing or the things that pull me
In a different direction.

You put my fears to rest as you put me first.
It is that which I can hardly believe
But some inadequacies loom.
I wish to fill the whole spectrum
Yet I may not.

Fear of the unknown is a powerful force
But why can I not use the strengths you have afforded me
To look at the future in the eye?

And as I close mine in the pursuit of comfort sleep provides
I am open to the prospect of
Together...forever
As one.

September 22, 1997

At Times Like These

At times like these
I learn the value of being loved,
The strength of a relationship,
And the "support of a good woman."

I can't think of only me
For you have feelings and desires and expectations,
But the load you now carry
May prove too heavy.

I shall understand if you drop it.
Because life is too short
And you deserve everything
And I can't provide it all.

I need help.
I need reassurance.
I need you.
But because I love you so much
I refuse to hold you back.

October 3, 1997

The Measure of a Man

I have learned from you
The measure of man
Is not in his ability to do
But his capacity to love.
You have made me a man.

December 3, 1997

Time

Proclaimed by many as the enemy
But not by me,
It has delivered me so much
This past year: a cure of your past
And of mine.
Thankfully it does heal all wounds.
It allowed us the opportunity
To explore ourselves and each other.
For only time may tell, I said
As the dangling intangibles drifted away
So the clock starts ticking now
Giving us time to love and live…
Together.
And at times like these
Time is on our side
Just as you are in my heart
Which is beating…beating
Knowing it is only a matter of time before
Our hearts shall beat as one
Till death do us part.

December 20, 1997

Thanks for Being You

I went to a distant land and was compelled
To partake in games well beyond the realm of my skills.
Yet, I emerged victorious and you reap the benefits herein.

A friend of mine once told me if you give a girl a gift
You should never have to sign it, because if she
Doesn't know who it is from it doesn't matter anyway.
Besides it can always keep them guessing.

All I can ask is that you please accept this.
You deserve this and much more because you are one
Of the most fascinating individual I have ever had
The pleasure of meeting. Thanks for being you.

1997

Love

Once something unobtainable, even undesirable,
Due to fear of commitment, fear of uncertainty,
Fear of vulnerability, fear of rejection.
Yet, this love leads to great anticipation,
Which delivers a sense of being, a sense of freedom,
And a sense of awareness.
Was it love at first sight? Unlikely.
It stems from unprecedented reflection, contemplation,
A myriad of thoughts culminating to an ultimate conclusion.

Love has found a home in me.
But it brings uncertainty and potential devastation.
Years of search have ended with a moment's reflection,
A derisive process becomes a uniqueness so compelling,
A fulfillment so rewarding.
Yet I am vulnerable.

It was an uncaring life which begat this cautious philosophy.
Caution has become a new turn, with an alternative and unfamiliar
    concept.
I am afraid of saying or doing the wrong thing,
Afraid of being misunderstood when likely I am not.

Presently a neophyte, this love seeks a mutual
Understanding, a mutual acknowledgement
This love compares only to a dream.
But with a word I could be so easily awakened.

1997

My Philosophy

My philosophies must be examined for continuation.
There are many yet by means of unruly articulation they are
    misunderstood.
These are philosophies of monogamy, trust, kindness, understanding,
Openness and caring.
One has surfaced above all others: a philosophy of love.
It is unfortunate this has been within, till now,
For it cannot be unveiled in an instant for fear you
May not believe it, or worse, that you may not accept it.

Who has earned this love?
Whom do I worship with limitless devotion?
Someone of principle.
Someone with a great sense of honesty, morals, and direction,
Direction which leads to goals, goals which in turn lead to a fulfilling life,
A life which I long to share.
You admit weaknesses, but they are dispelled by every breath you take.
You have brought life to someone who has been emotionally dead.
I have been born again with a new sense of pride, awareness,
And greatest of all, a new sense of purpose.
At the lowest point of my life you have raised me to a new height.
A wise friend of mine once said I "must experience the depths of life before
    I can
Discover the heights. "
You have cast out my depths and granted me this height.
You are so easy to relate to yet so uneasily discernable.
You know love, I think, this defeats me, but you may lose again, of that I'm
    sure.
Your strengths shall cure my weakness.
Your devotion to your philosophies shall enable me to be dogmatic.
Your common sense shall give birth to my logic.
Your presence shall uplift my character.
I love you with all my heart.

1997

IV

Truth

The line between truth and fiction
Is as translucent as thought itself.
One can be too honest,
With the inevitable results.
We should not share every thought
In word.
We should not bare our soul
In weakness.
We should not get discarded
By truth.
We deserve our private thoughts
And desires and motivations.
I have never felt so bare,
And shall not again.
However, the truth shall not die,
But it won't be cut to the bone either.

March 19, 1998

Stages

I have travelled the world of thought
Not in eighty days, but in eighty hours
And what a journey it has been.
Beginning with relief as some responsibility has vanished,
Then pounded by the sense of loss,
Remorse and failure.
I wanted to turn around and beg for another chance
But landed at the destination called reality.
Why had relief been the first leg of the journey?
I knew why,
But I was beginning to forget.
I lost myself
Just as I was discovering who I am.
I played at a level I could not sustain.
One cannot be rooted in the ground
And play with the stars.
You have to travel there in…
Stages.

March 19, 1998

Just Right

I laughed as I pondered
My relationships past.
I feel like Goldilocks
Because one was too cold,
One was too hot,
So I shall seek the one just right.

March 19, 1998

The Perfect One

I hope you find what you seek
Making the best of what comes
Along in the meantime,
Giving your all
In search of getting the same,
Needing to fulfill your dream
And knowing time is running out.
To compromise would be
Inconceivable since surely the
Perfect one is out there when in fact he is
Not.

Because I believe he can only be found
In your imagination.

March 19, 1998

Once Again

I recall once saying
I was the right guy at the right time for you
And believed that to be true.
Just as I recall the day I was not.
It was long ago,
And I should have told you,
But me of all people thought I could change.
I recognized your needs
And who was right for you
And because I could not admit it wasn't me
I wasted so many months of your life.
Go seek.
I fear you shall not find.
However, you are one step closer
By shedding me
And availing yourself once again.

March 19, 1998

Praying for the Storm

The swirling and churning
That has become my mantle
Has me out of control,
Assuming I had it.
This mantle has things in order
All placed where they should.
But as I examine them
They represent only chaos
And as I examine the eye
Where all too infrequently I reside
It is not long enough or sustainable.
I move out of it as quickly and with ease
As I enter.
Only I understand and only I can alter it.
Life has eliminated my capacity
For a balanced mantle.
Yet as I stare at it
I am praying for the storm
That once brought me the opportunity
And delivered me the peace
I crave,
But fail to seek.

May 30, 1998

Why Can't I?

A son, a father, a lover, a life.
Everyone else is coping with these.
Why can't I?
Where is the balance?
I have all the tools,
But they are scattered on the floor
And as I blindly search around
I come up empty handed
Or choose the wrong one.
Everyone else just follows the manual.
Why can't I?
It's functional,
Which is good enough for me,
But it breaks down so easily
And I can only fix it so many times.
It becomes high maintenance
If it is not fixed from the beginning.
As I see it,
There are just too many moving parts to deal with,
So store it away, for now.
Everyone else moves on.
Why can't I?

May 30, 1998

Faith

I had one of those rare quiet moments
Alone in my thoughts,
The ones full of you and only you.

Yet, I am never alone
Because you fill up my being
Like a religion.

And as with all faiths,
It is tested from time to time.
I have my doubts today.
And I fear
All that shall remain
Are pictures in a book,
Corners in a mind,
Flashes of a past,

And the creations of an atheist.

August 26, 1998

Blessed

You are,
Therefore, I am.

You are an inspiration,
And I am inspired.

You are intelligent,
And I am brighter for having known you.

You are driven,
And I am in awe.

You are gentle,
And I am rewarded.

You are forgiving,
So I may be human.

You are loving,
And I am blessed.

Blessed for who you are
And therefore,

I am.

August 26, 1998

Soul

I realized today
A soul is not what lifts,
Greeting God,
As one's breath draws silent.

It is created and nourished…
In love.

And if you haven't touched someone's life
And allowed him or her to touch yours,

You have no soul.

For it's "soul" in "mate"
That defines the spirit.

And as wondrous as the creation is,
And as elusive as the maintenance is,
It's separation that tears at your very essence,
Weakens your vigilance,
And puts your soul to rest.

December 9, 1998

A Tear

A tear quietly graced my cheek
And as this outward drop has its cause,
It forces me to look inward
And ask tough questions.

I brushed it aside,
Yet I cannot brush aside the impact,
The remorse,
The what if's.

All I feel is dismay
For what can I offer the future?
I have so little to give
And even less desire to give it.

The lonely tear shall represent the lonely man.
For inward I'll turn
As inward I look
Remembering…

How little I gave
And how much I took.

December 21, 1998

Christmas Dreams

for Holly

A Christmas of dreams would be one spent
In your home,
In your arms,
In your heart.
So this one is special, above all others,
For it is the last.

And as we drift…but not too far,
And as we move on…but not too quickly,
And as we fade…but not to black,
I am left with only dreams…

Of our home,
Of our embrace,
Of our love.

1998

Waiting

Waiting by a phone,
    that isn't going to ring.

Waiting for a car,
    that isn't going to stop.

Waiting for a kiss,
    that isn't even a thought.

Waiting for a love,
    too distant to even be a memory.

Waiting for an opportunity,
    to never miss an opportunity
    like this again.

December 23, 1998

A Story Book Finish

I have wrapped myself in fiction
For the last couple of years.
Drawn into the plot,
    Tear by tear,
    Smile by smile,
    Touch by touch.

But as I read on a little further,
I learned…
    You can't lean on the wind.
    You can't fit into a dream.
    You can't speak out of turn.

So as the plot sickened,
And as the final bags were dropped off,
    There were no breezes blowing,
    The nightmare was beginning,
    And the silence was deafening.

December 28, 1998

Any Addiction

Like any other addiction,
As each day passes

You think of it a little less,
You need it a little less,
You want it a little less.

Victory arrives only
When your first thought of the day
      Is of something else,
And when you complete a thought
      That does not include her,
And you look out a window
      Without her reflection,
And you hear a certain song
      Without asking by whom,
And you drive a certain road
      With only the journey in mind.

It is not a victory yet.
But, I can see the podium off in the distance.

December 29, 1998

Trust

The last two years were
A victory of sorts.

When I came to you,
You had it all…

      But trust.

And as your teary recollections
Fell on my shoulder,
That night, you were human.

I knew the job I had to do.

So…   I never lied,
        I never misled you,
        I never judged.

And as you walk away,
Thinking you wasted your time,

Without you even knowing,

I gave you back
Something only time could buy.
And I could sell:

      Trust.

December 30, 1998

Then and Now

Compare, if you will,
The way you came into this
And the way you have left.

Sure, you became frustrated,
With bags too heavy to carry
And considering
What you had to work with.

But you were barely functioning.
Now you at least have resolve.

So as your journey continues,
In the absence of me
You at least have healed,

We must agree.

December 30, 1998

Fate

I bet you thought fate
Would put a shovel back in my hand.
It is not to be,
As I dig myself out of the emotional
Avalanche I am barely surviving.

The snow that gave us another chance
Serves as warning this time.
Trusting I get the drift,
Rather than pushing it to the side.

I am as scattered as the flakes in air.
But, as they land, some stability ensues.
So I'll stay on the ground
Till fate melts away.

January 3, 1999

The Road, So Long

I knew where I was going.
That is, I knew how to get there.
But the shortest journey
Is not always the straightest line.

I had to pull over from time to time.
And falling behind
Was a consequence with which to reckon.

I had to take some side roads
For fear of discovery,
And to recharge my batteries.

And as I announced the destination
We slowed to a halt.
And as the door slammed
There was only enough time

To say farewell
To the road,
So long.

January 12, 1999

Stranger

Don't be a stranger
You said.
And it struck me,
I am a stranger within myself.
So as this journey begins,
Neigh, continues,
It must be completed.
And should our paths cross,
I hope I am complete.
For you have built me,
Painstaking piece by piece.
You deserve to see the finished product,
But I have a long way to go,
And how can I get there
When, as you know,
We are not supposed to talk to strangers?

April 19, 1999

Breath of Fresh Air

You are like a breath of fresh air.
And as I inhale,
You fill my thoughts
Till I get a little giddy.

For it has been some time
Since I felt this relaxed,
And this focused,
And this out of breath.

April 27, 1999

Pleasure

I feel like a kid again,
Perhaps for the first time.

You grant me this pleasure
With your laughter,
Your expressions,
Your warmth.

I love this feeling
Because it is so new
And fresh
And wonderful.

The best part is,
For the first time
In a long time,

I don't want to escape.

May 8, 1999

Because

I held your hand today,
Because I didn't have to.

I looked up into your eyes,
Because I didn't have to.

I ran with you,
I shared in your laughter,
And tasted the softness of your lips,
Because I didn't have to.

I touched your hair,
And you touched my heart.

I could not stop thinking of you today
Because…

May 8, 1999

My Hearth

I thought my heart could only be dragged back
Kicking and screaming
Keeping the hearth cold and empty.

But somehow,
You have spun it around,
And given it a tug,
And pulled it in the right direction.

In its new life,
The beat shall be gradual,
The joy shall be genuine,
And the fulfillment complete.

As caution covers its mantle,
You feed the fire
With the fuel of who you are.

So as the ambers glow,
And the beating quickens,
And the life rushes back,

I feel myself warming by it,
Reveling in it.

Mesmerized by your flame.

May 9, 1999

Know

Though you are halfway 'round the world,
Know a second of my thoughts bring you back.

And as you waken for your day,
Know I dream of you in my night.

And as the sun sets in your sky,
Know it wakens me,
       And you are my first thought.

And as the stars fill your night,
Know my day is empty without you.

And as you sleep in your pleasant dreams,
Know I watch over you in my mind's eye.

And as you return,
Know in my heart

       You never left.

May 25, 1999

Oasis

You are my oasis
So as I cross the dunes
And gaze upon your wonders
They are not so distant.

My thirst for you grows
As I crawl ever closer
Knowing my search is over,
Knowing at last I may drink.

So as I reach your water's edge
I can only marvel in the discovery
That it is not just a pool of your love
I have found.

It is an ocean

And it is real.

July 23, 1999

Senses

If I lost my eyesight,
My mind's eye would draw you in.

If I lost my hearing,
I could watch your moving lips
As they pledge your love.

If I lost my sense of touch,
Your roaming fingers would not be lost on my soul.

If I lost my sense of taste,
Your presence would feed my desire.

If I lost my sense of smell,
Your essence would echo in my mind.

If I lost my mind,
Your spirit would will me back.

If I lost you,
My senses would serve no purpose.

September 7, 1999

Thoughts

You are the last thought of every day
And the first of each morning.

I cannot share them with you
And create a distance.

I cannot act
And create a void.

I wish I could see you each day,
Rather than drawing you in from the mind's eye.
But patience looms large once again,
And destiny needs not only a hand
But a timetable,

And a generous one at that.

So thoughts become simple reminders
And no longer anticipation
Of events which may unfold,

But remain for now only thoughts.

October 13, 1999

Written Over Time

"I love you with all of my heart"
Or so the saying goes,
Somehow seems inadequate
In describing how I feel.

So, I reach for words,
And try to gather them up,
Somehow forming a sentence.

Yet, it cannot be done.
For a sentence, a verse, a novel, an epic
Proves insufficient to express these thoughts of love.

This is simply innate.
It is a sense of being.
It cannot be justified with a pen.

Only written over time.

The best part is…
We will not be reading about it.

We shall be living it.

December 24, 1999

Loving Kim

And what of loving Kim,
Wonder I.

One's heart soars from the wings of her affection.
One's soul climbs from the mountains of her virtue.
One's mind is a pool in the ocean of her intellect.
One's passion quivers from the arrows of her lust.
One's body is whole from the gift of her being.
One's heart bleeds from the daggers of her absence.
One's spirit lifts from the winds of her return.

September 10, 2000

A Gift

You have come to me as a gift
Like a Russian doll.

I have opened it piece by piece with the wonder of a child.
Peeking at first,
Then hurriedly searching for the core,
And marvelling as each new layer reveals
A greater treasure,
A more precious find,
Then a core of satisfaction and contentment.

I view it from all sides
Finally clutching it to my heart.

This gift is of who you are
Yet the real gift is that

You have allowed me to be myself.

September 13, 2000

Day Dreams

I day dream about you
Lost in this love
As no real thoughts are formed.
It's just a haze, a warm blanket of
Contentment, joy and tranquillity.
Drifting in and out
For no apparent reason.
It is how day dreams should be.
And life has become.

    I love you.

February 15, 2001

For the Moment

It strikes me often
In this new life
The feeling of comfort and contentment.

It feels secure and good.

The moment does not build,
It simply is,
Tickling my conscience
Till it gets my attention
And helps me realize
How good life can be
For the moment
And…
For a lifetime.

June 17, 2001

Away

When you are away
I can only form half of my thoughts.

When you are away
My fragmented soul cannot soar.

When you are away
My will is a fraction of its strength.

When you are away
My spirit is a shadow of its former self.

When you are away
I simply wait to rebuild.

When you are home…

I am complete.

August 20, 2002

More and More

I wish you could see yourself from my point of view from time to time.

You are generous to a fault with your time, expertise and caring.

I love you for your generosity.

I wish you knew how your funny little expressions lift one's spirit and spark a laugh after you have done something wrong or bought something for yourself.

I love you for your expressions.

I wish you knew how patient you are, considering all of the challenges you have taken on in the last six years.

I love you for your patience.

I wish you could be there when I revisit a moment when you were funny.

I love you for your sense of humour.

What I love the most is that you DO know these things, but are far too humble to admit.

I love you for your modesty.

Perhaps you have helped me realize that being in love with you is not about the impact on me.

Who could not love YOU, with all you have to give?

I love you for you.

More and more…

July 16, 2005

ACKNOWLEDGEMENTS

First and foremost to my wife, Kimberly. Words cannot convey the degree of gratitude I have for you. You have raised my three children, while successfully building a career and your own consulting business. You have been my primary caregiver, and as my Parkinson's Disease worsens and my care needs increase you continue to be my rock. This book would not have been published without your support. I am thankful for your honesty, integrity, and commitment to my family and me.

I would like to thank my nephew Aaron Bethune for his expertise, insight, and leadership in putting together the volume of life as I have seen it. I would also like to thank my editor, Lorraine Gane, Laura Lavender for her artwork and hand-lettering, and Clint Hutzulak for his graphic design work. It takes a village.

ABOUT THE AUTHOR

Paul Bethune was born in Kingston, Ontario, in 1958, to a Navy family. After a number of moves in his early childhood, his father retired, and the family settled in Ancaster, where he was raised in a comfortable, middle-class home.

Paul now lives in Toronto with his wife, Kimberly Robinson. He was diagnosed with Parkinson's disease in 2011 and has been retired since. He continues to be an avid golfer, despite mobility challenges and an increasingly disappointing handicap. He has three adult children: Courtland, Emma-Lee, and Lane. They lead full, successful lives nearby, and visit often, enriching their parents' lives. A full life — however, a grandchild, or two, would be a nice addition.

CPSIA information can be obtained
at www.ICGtesting.com
Printed in the USA
LVHW092257230719
625117LV00003B/19/P

9 780993 636738